T0316253

ALEXANDRE DUMAS [Père]

THE TOWER

[La Tour de Nesle]

or *Marguerite de Bourgogne*

IN A NEW VERSION FROM THE FRENCH BY

CHARLES WOOD

OBERON BOOKS
LONDON

This translation first published by Oberon Books Ltd,
521 Caledonian Road, London N7 9RH

Tel: 0171 607 3637/Fax 0171 607 3629

ISBN: 9781870259606

Cover design: Andrzej Klimowski

For my brother Peter
once a true swashbuckler

INTRODUCTION

NICHOLAS DROMGOOLE

Alexandre Dumas, born in 1802, had a parentage that seems almost too aptly prepared for the Romantic Movement. His father had been a general, a contemporary of Napoleon, in the French Revolutionary army, his grandfather a French aristocrat, his grandmother a black slave in San Domingo - even Lord Byron's background seems positively pallid in comparison. In the annals of French literature, the Alexandre Dumas who wrote *The Three Musketeers* and *The Tower* is known as Dumas Père, because his illegitimate son Dumas Fils, became in his turn the celebrated author of *La Dame aux Camelias*.

By the time he wrote *The Three Musketeers* in 1845, still undoubtedly his best known novel, and still very much in print, Dumas Père had become not so much an individual writer as almost an industry, and it is still debatable just how much that book owes to the efforts of others. It is based, event by event and far too closely for artistic respectability, on *The Memoirs of Monsieur d'Artagnon, Capitaine-Lieutenant of The First Company of The King's Musketeers* by Gatien de Courtilz, published in 1700. A record is kept in the Marseilles library that Dumas took the book out in 1843 and never returned it. Even so he collaborated closely with Auguste Maquet on the book. To be fair, when

Dumas had previously wanted to acknowledge another such collaboration, his publisher refused. 'Anything signed Alexandre Dumas is worth three francs a line - sign it Dumas and Maquet and it won't fetch thirty sous a line.'

Naturally as Dumas became ever more famous, his collaborators resented their anonymity. In 1845 a pamphlet attacking him was published entitled *Manufacture Of Romantic Novels - The Firm of Alexandre Dumas and Co.*, purporting to tell all.

So it is not surprising to learn that *The Tower*, written in 1832, and Dumas' most famous play, also had similarly murky origins. It was based on a play by an aspiring writer, Frederick Gaillardet, who had given his manuscript to Harel, the manager of the Theatre de la Porte-Saint-Martin, where Dumas had already had great success with his historical melodrama, *Anthony*, in 1831. Harel first asked the critic, Janin, to attempt a re-write, but then asked Dumas to see what he could do with the play. Still on a sick bed after a cholera epidemic, Dumas duly 'improved' the play, and even generously offered to take only a fee, leaving the authorship to Gaillardet alone. Harel preferred to advertise the play as by a set of asterisks and Frederick Gaillardet, and then after suitable haggling, agreed with Gaillardet to put the young man's name first, and then the asterisks. He then busily spread the real name of the second author by word of mouth. The play was a great success, and Dumas henceforward insisted on including it in any list of his own works. Ultimately he and Gaillardet fought a duel, pistols not swords, over Gaillardet's claim

that the play was really his. Neither managed to hit
the other. The play continued a hit for 800 perform-
ances and was constantly revived. Years later
Gaillardet asked that the name of Dumas should be
coupled with his at a revival in recognition of 'the
large part his incomparable talent had in the success
of the play.' Posterity has been unkind to
Gaillardet. There is no doubt we now think of the
play as belonging very much to Dumas; and like
the whole tribe of the other collaborators of
Dumas, Gaillardet has largely sunk from sight.

Scurrilous pamphlets, duels, rival claims from
disgruntled collaborators, none of these affected
Dumas' growing reputation, nor his ever increasing
public. Dumas learned his trade as a writer in the
competitive and demanding world of the
commercial theatre. He began by writing for
vaudeville, but just as Hector Berlioz was over-
whelmed by the visit of an English theatre
company playing Shakespeare to Paris in 1829,
they inspired his *Symphony Fantastique*, so they
opened up fresh vistas for Dumas as well. Berlioz
fell even more heavily for a young actress in the
company, Harriet Smithson, than he did for
Shakespeare, marrying her in 1833 and emerging
disillusioned from their relationship nine years
later, but with his allegiance to Shakespeare
undimmed. Dumas had the artistic acumen and
imagination to realise that the new romanticism
and historical drama were made for each other, and
his *Henri III et sa Cour* 1829, was perhaps the first
triumph of Romantic theatre. This alongside other
plays by Dumas busily scurrying back down the
corridors of time for sensation and scandal, put him

at the forefront of the Romantic movement, and brought him the friendship and admiration of Alfred de Vigny and Victor Hugo.

Recognising the creation of a new French theatrical genre - historical melodrama - Dumas, on a rising tide of affluence, built and financed the Theatre Historique, but like so many creative artists, his ambitions outreached his grasp of finance, and continually in debt in spite of his huge earnings, he saw his creation fail in 1850. Yet throughout his literary career he never deserted the theatre. Better known in the twentieth century for his novels, in fact he wrote almost a hundred plays, even turning many of his novels into subsequent plays. Even as a novelist he never lost sight of the theatre's immediacy, his effects are largely theatrical effects, one almost hears at the end of a chapter the audience's sudden gasp of surprise at the final twist, the last effective line before the curtain trundles down. It was not where he got his material, nor who assembled it for him, so much as what Dumas did with it that mattered. The name of Dumas was worth three francs a line because his touch was unique. 'Nobody had read every Dumas book or seen every Dumas play, that would be almost as impossible as for any one person to have written every Dumas book and play - but everybody had read some Dumas.' - 'If a Robinson Crusoe exists in 1850 he must surely be about to read *The Three Musketeers*.' - 'The world, including France, learned its French history from Dumas.' 'Does Dumas make you think? Hardly ever. Dream? Never. But turn page after compulsive page? Always!'

He was the great populariser of Romanticism. This new movement in art turned it's back on the industrial revolution, then transforming the cities in which the artists of Romanticism actually lived, as they sought excitement in tear-jerking emotions, sentimental love at first sight, the macabre, the frightening and the supernatural, indeed almost anything that got away from the present - other cultures, other times, from medieval Scotland and oriental fantasy to historical romance.

The very industrialism that art largely ignored created a new middle - class audience, richer but far less discriminating and less demanding than the smaller more exclusively educated class an author could expect in the previous century. Dumas was writing for a mass readership, the first in history, and he gave them colourful, exciting heroics dressed up in the trappings of the past. *The Tower* is a prime example of what became for him a well tried formula.

One of the first questions today's audience will want answered is just how true to the actual historical facts as we know them, is the account given by Dumas. It is one thing for Shakespeare, in the name of dramatic licence, to massage and manipulate events and people into an order acceptable within the confines of the stage, the three to four hours of the performance, and the limits of the dramatically possible. With the understandable exception of *Richard III*, Shakespeare gave his audience a set of guidelines to enable them to understand and appreciate what had actually happened in the past. In his historical plays he was recreating a sense of national identity from a re-telling of events that were much closer to real life than to myth. Dumas was doing nothing so acceptable. He was re-writing, creating a set of bogus events, that bore almost no relation at all to the actual facts that history recorded, and his aim was to sensationalise, to startle his audience with horrific scandals and events.

It is true that the prestige of the French throne at the beginning of the fourteenth century was affected by the scandals associated with Philip the Fair's three daughters in law, Marguerite of Burgundy [married to the future Louis X], Jeanne of Poitiers [married to the future Philip V] and Blanche of the Marche [married to the future Charles IV]. Jeanne's innocence was established and proclaimed by a Parlement, but Blanche and Marguerite were convicted of having had as lovers two gentlemen in waiting, Philippe and Gaultier d'Aulnay, who were duly excecuted. The two princesses were imprisoned in solitary confinement in the Chateau Gaillard. In due course Blanche entered a nunnery. Marguerite became an embarrassment when her husband later mounted the throne and wished to marry Clementia, daughter of the King of Hungary. Rather than face long drawn out negotiations with the papacy for a royal divorce, Louis X had his wife smothered in her cell between two mattresses. How enthusiastic his second wife was to ally herself to such a Bluebeard, history has not recorded, although Louis X was known to his people as Louis the Quarrelsome. Not the sort of husband a wife was likely to pick a quarrel with.

This incident, a royal princess committing adultery with a courtier, has been inflated by Dumas in *The Tower* into an astounding series of events. Marguerite, presented as queen, has had two children by a former lover. He re-appears and blackmails her into giving him high office, but both are unaware that the two children, far from being put to death, are in fact none other than the two gentlemen in waiting, Philippe and Gaultier d'Aulnay, who both die in suitably lurid circumstances with a great deal of the nineteenth century equivalent of tomato ketchup liberally bedaubing everything and everyone in sight.

As with farce, to which it is closely allied, melodrama is a theatrical genre which develops its own conventions. Characters are simplified and exaggerated, the good are absurdly good, and in just as much caricature, the bad are unbelievably bad. To be effective the genre requires a swift moving plot, full of unexpected twists and turns. It may be almost impossible to believe moments such as:

> [*Enter GAULTIER covered in blood*]
> GAULTIER
> Marguerite... I give you back the
> key to the Tower...
> MARGUERITE
> Gaultier, I am your mother.
> GAULTIER
> My mother? My mother?
> [*Horror - his hand and arm out to curse her*]
> Then be dammed!
> [*GAULTIER dies*]

But the swift moving narrative, dealing out fresh surprises in spades, obviously carried it's nineteenth century audience inexorably onwards and away into a never-never land of thrills and fantasy.

Even in the brief extract above, one virtue of the play as presented here is very clear. Charles Wood's lean, rhythmic language makes the most of the drama and of Dumas [if indeed it is Dumas and not Gaillardet], and loses none of the fun.

For a modern audience scenes like these are hard to take. Already by the 1890's Wilde could say of Dickens that 'it took a heart of stone not to laugh at little Nell'. Whereas Dickens still succeeds as a writer at a variety of levels, even if his sentimentality can seem mawkish, Dumas seems less rich. At the level of exciting boys' adventure stories his books and plays still work - Dumas actually took one of his plots from Fenimore Cooper - but these days an adult readership expects a more perceptive approach to characters than Dumas' broad outlines of people. Rather than developing, changing, being affected by events and maturing as they interact with one another, Dumas' characters tend to remain the same from beginning to end. They are goodies and baddies at the start and they come to their inevitable good or bad end at the finish with a certain predictability. It is, to use Coleridge's term, difficult to suspend our disbelief.

It is only with an indulgent smile at the excesses of mid-nineteenth century melodrama, once beloved by its less demanding audience, but now impossibly dated, that we can span the gap between ourselves and the different expectations of over 160 years ago. This only applies to melodrama. We are not, as yet, cut off to the same extent from a whole range of other Victorian arts, but we have lost their taste, in that first flush of Romanticism, for melodrama. Dumas began in the theatre where melodrama then reigned supreme, and the sure knowledge of what would 'go with the public', of exactly what they wanted, was once his main strength. Paradoxically, to some, it is now his weakness. Melodrama is out of fashion. Yet perhaps if we *can* learn to view these cardboard heroes of outdated fiction with that indulgent smile, we will realise the very solid virtues Dumas still possesses. The fun and excitement of a fast moving story, a boyish enthusiasm for heroes and bravery which never quite leaves any of us, the deft turn and turn about of a plot that is still easy to follow, the colour and romance of a nostalgic past.

Even today whenever the weather gets rough at sea, the Greek fisherman of Lemnos, hoping to calm the evil spirit of Alexander the Great's mother, thought to be blindly seeking her son in the heart of the storm, shout into the wind 'Alexander still lives.'

Through all the vicissitudes of changing fashion as the years have hurtled by Alexandre Dumas still lives too, books in print, plays still performed. Audience's perceptions and expectations may have changed but in Dumas' works too, at the heart of the Romantic storm, something is still very much alive.

London 1995

THE TOWER

CHARACTERS

MARGUERITE DE BOURGOGNE

BURIDAN

GAULTIER D'AULNAY

PHILIPPE D'AULNAY

ORSINI

LANDRY

SAVOISY

DE PIERREFONDS

DE MARIGNY

LOUIS X

RAOUL

CHARLOTTE

VEILED WOMAN

NECROMANCER

POURSUIVANT at ARMS

SERGEANT

ARBALÉTRIER

BOATMAN

JEHAN

RICHARD

SIMON

Guards, Courtiers, Lords, Petitioners

The action of the play takes place in Paris in 1314

This version of *The Tower* was first performed by the Almeida Theatre Company, at the Almeida Theatre, London on 8th December, 1995, in a production directed by Howard Davies with the following cast:

MARGUERITE DE BOURGOGNE, Sinead Cusack
BURIDAN, Adrian Dunbar
GAULTIER D'AULNAY, Ben Miles
PHILIPPE D'AULNAY, John Light
ORSINI, David Herlihy
LANDRY, Nigel Lindsay
SAVOISY, Geoffrey Beevers
DE PIERREFONDS, Tim McMullan
DE MARIGNY/LOUIS X, Iain Mitchell
RAOUL, Hugh Simon
CHARLOTTE, Cate Hamer
SIMON, Perry Benson
RICHARD, Gregory Donaldson
AN ARBALÉTRIER , Derren Litten
JEHAN/OLIVIER/POURSUIVANT AT ARMS,
Michael Hodgson

DIRECTION: Howard Davies
DESIGN: John Napier
LIGHTING: Mark Henderson
MUSIC: Jonathan Dove
FIGHTS: William Hobbs
SOUND: John A Leonard

ACT ONE

The curtain rises

SCENE 1

The banks of the River Seine

[*Double tower of the Tour de Nesle, a hidden quay and steps up from the river. City wall. Gate of Saint-Honore. Boats*]

[*Heard off: Fanfare. Drums, trumpets, bagpipes and cymbals. Clamour of horse, foot, shout*]

[*Civic entry of MARGUERITE DE BOURGOGNE, soon to be Queen of France. Horses, lances, banners shadows across the scene. A crescendo of noise and then fading*]

[*Enter PHILIPPE D'AULNAY, a young squire from the Flanders war - gambeson, white cross of France, belt, sword, dagger and purse, hose, short boots, spurs - excited by what he's seen*]

[*Enter a VEILED WOMAN*]

VEILED WOMAN
Mon jeune seigneur!

PHILIPPE
Oui?

VEILED WOMAN
I must speak secretly.

PHILIPPE
I cannot hear, drums, music still
in my ears. Our Queen has entered
Paris and I have just seen her, my
brother, Gaultier at her side.

Him, I could not see for bright
steel, gold, silver... sumpture.

But side her he rode, captain of
her guard... I... I... am come to
Paris... for good or ill.

[*The clamour fades*]

Proud queen... I know she saw me.
[*He strikes a pose*]
"I've caught her eyes. All must
exclaim: the loveliest heard or
seen is she!"

[*The procession has gone*]

There, what do you say to that?
[*Laughing, he beckons*]
I can hear you now, whatever you
would say... say it.
[*He listens to her*]
Oh! *Oui, oui*... I am?

I am sure that I am and if she is
beautiful...?
[*He listens affronted*]
Woman! I never break a *rendezvous*,
desert a friend, refuse a breach or
disappoint a lady does me honour...

VEILED WOMAN
Your hand! A man will ask to see
your hand...
[*She gives him something*]
...on which... this ring.

PHILIPPE
Merci, ma gracieuse.

VEILED WOMAN
Adieu mon soldat!
[*Going*] *Plaisir et courage!*

[*Exit VEILED WOMAN. PHILIPPE laughs*]

PHILIPPE

Eh bien.

First I shall write to my brother.

[*Exit PHILIPPE*]

[*A shout from the city wall, an ARBALÉTRIER (cross-bow-man) in his pepperpot or sentry box*]

ARBALÉTRIER
There floats another!

[*Enter SERGEANT, in a boat with two BOATMEN*]

SERGEANT
There!
[*To BOATMEN*]
See it .. your hooks.

[*Leaping ashore, and the ARBALÉTRIER down from his pepperpot, they drag out the body of a young man by way of the steps and the quay*]

ARBALÉTRIER
Find more. It is always three.

[*He crosses himself*]

SERGEANT
You are safe for your vile visage.
[*Back in the boat*]
Oui... *la lune* .. see it? Another
pretty young man... see it, get
out to it... *un fleurant... un*
vasistas... oh shameful, wasteful.

BOATMAN
It will not escape us...
[*Rowing*] ...it is rare they swim with
throats cut - not even fish.

[*ARBALÉTRIER drags away the slime wet dead body of the young man who is without his hose, throat cut*]

[*Exit SERGEANT and BOATMEN in boat*]

SCENE 2

Orsini's tavern at the gate of Saint Honore

[*PHILIPPE writing at a table. The tavern full. The pot boy LANDRY, JEHAN. Shoemaker, RICHARD with SIMON a fisherman, both have had a lot of wine. ORSINI serving OTHERS, stopped by them*]

SIMON

The count?

ORSINI

What?

SIMON

Drowned rats this morning?

RICHARD

I said he was to ask Orsini because
if 'tis to do with the devil he
will know...

ORSINI

Three.

RICHARD

I said he would know, it would
surprise me not if...

SIMON

All noble, young and pretty?

RICHARD

...he pushed them in. He is evil
is Orsini - say so, say... Evil?

ORSINI

Three fine young men, good names,
comely, less than a week in Paris.

RICHARD

It is always the same. I swear he
poisons them. Orsini?

ORSINI

I do not.

SIMON

One thing... the devil, whoever
the devil is, and he is a devil to
spill young blood, this - he knows
who to pick.

RICHARD:

Oui.
[*Savouring*]
The highest in the land, their very
fruit of their very loins - tender
necks ripped open and slid into the
Seine...

ORSINI

That is truth.

RICHARD

...and... all in the same stretch
of river, below the Tower of Nesle.

ORSINI

That is truth. Will you drink
more?

RICHARD

I will do... but who? Who does it

to these poor young valiant pretty
young fish?

ORSINI

I know not.

SIMON

You know not?
Orsini you know everything filthy
and evil, poisonous, malodorous,
diabolical, shunned by polite
Christians... you are familiar in
every way for, you... know witches,
consort with them - suck their paps...
paps...
[*Loves the thought*] ...paps.

PHILIPPE

Mâitre!

ORSINI

I know nothing.

SIMON

Nothing? I know you ought answer
that young man does you the honour.
I myself would not be so...

PHILIPPE

Mâitre!
[*Indicating the letter he writes*]

SIMON

...civil, but then...

ORSINI

Messire?

SIMON

...I know you.

PHILIPPE

One of your pot boys... I shall
give him a sou will he take this
for me... two?

[*PHILIPPE signs the letter with a flourish, a grin at ORSINI*]

ORSINI

Landry!

[*LANDRY, a huge brute of a man, quondam sergeant, tattered quilted jacket with faded white cross, an arbalétrier's belt with spanning hook, a double dagger sheath, footless and dangling separate hose, bare feet - has lurked, listening*]

LANDRY:

Sous parisis?

PHILIPPE

Oui...

ORSINI

Take it.

RICHARD

I cannot believe him... I cannot
believe you Orsini.

ORSINI

I care not - what you believe.

[*PHILIPPE addresses the letter. LANDRY is waiting*]

SIMON

Was I foul named Orsini, tavern
keeper of a filthy tavern so close
to the old Tower of Nesle which it
is, I would know...

RICHARD

If I had windows looked out, as
yours do Orsini, I would only need
look out at night and see every
thing in the river, slid in...

SIMON

I would have no surprise you have
plucked a few purses out, looped to

belts strapped about fine rich
pretty young drowned fish *first*,
Orsini, before any with boat and
grapple, for you are a very evil
very sly Italy villain.

ORSINI

I am not a villain. Nor of the
night watch...

RICHARD

The devil you are a villain!

ORSINI

I am an innkeeper.

SIMON

Then, as well, go to him - the
devil!

ORSINI

On instant you let go me I shall.
Do you want more wine?

SIMON

Yes I do want more wine. At once!

[*SIMON tosses down a coin. ORSINI picks it up*]

ORSINI

Inside whose purse have you been
fishing?

[*ORSINI exits*]

SIMON

What! I am an honest man!

RICHARD

You are, Simon.

SIMON

Twice today I have been called
thief!

PHILIPPE
To my brother, at the Louvre, his
name... Gaultier d'Aulnay.

SIMON
You say his name?

[*LANDRY goes with the letter*]

PHILIPPE
You know him?

[*SIMON stands, sways slightly as if about to say something,
then sits down again, sniggers to RICHARD*]

SIMON
He asks do we know him?

RICHARD
Saw you the procession into Paris?

SIMON
You ask me, Richard?

PHILIPPE
The Queen... I saw.

RICHARD
With sisters, the Princesses Jeanne
and Blanche?

[*JEHAN joins them*]

SIMON
I saw it. He says, "I saw it..."

JEHAN:
[*Spits*] I saw it...

RICHARD:
You saw our taxes on the back of
the bitch's favourite, cloth of
gold, ribbons, Gaultier d'Aulnay?

SIMON
I saw him.

He saw not me, nor did his demon of
a horse... a caracole, paws up,
pied de boeuf, as if my hand, my
back, it would use to step up!

When I scream quarter, what is give
me?

JEHAN

Gold?

SIMON

Oui! Gold. A blow on my head from
the gold pommel of his sword and he
berates me a king of thieves!

JEHAN

What did you call him?

SIMON

Shoved my knife a full three inch
up his mare's arse and called him
bastard... *au trot!*

PHILIPPE

Who calls my brother, bastard?

SIMON

I do. For recent memory of him.

[*PHILIPPE throws his full goblet at* SIMON's *head*]

PHILIPPE

You lie in your throat, filth!

[*SIMON ducks the goblet. Out with his dagger, calls*]

SIMON

A moi! Les enfants... kill the
bastard's brother...

[*RICHARD and JEHAN and OTHERS, knives out, some ten
of them from various parts of the room rally to* SIMON]

OMNES

A moi! Kill the ponce...
the pretty boy... *la pisseuse...*

[PHILIPPE has drawn his sword]

PHILIPPE

See it?

Stand back! My tongue licks longer
than your knives - you are warned!

SIMON

We have ten blades to your one, you
die, *fleur... cul!*

PHILIPPE

I warn. Stand back.

RICHARD

Kill the silly little prick.

*[ALL form a circle around PHILIPPE. Each calls in turn:
"Here! Here! Monsieur!" PHILIPPE thrusts his sword as
they cry, thrusts and the MAN steps back, another calls
"Here!" and PHILIPPE thrusts then at him, who steps back;
the OTHERS, a closing circle of knives - closer and closer]*

*[Enter BURIDAN, richly dressed, mail, a surcoat with arms
of two nude women affronte in fess all enclosed in a
coronet about their waists, gold spurs, a sable trimmed
cape. He tosses the cape onto a table and draws his sword]*

BURIDAN

Brisons là! Enough! Five too many
for one gentleman... one... two...
three and - *à moi, à moi,* messire!

*[He wades into them, disdaining to use other than the flat
of his sword on their backs, until they break and PHILIPPE
and BURIDAN stand, swords on guard, shoulder to
shoulder]*

PHILIPPE

Messire?

BURIDAN

Messire?

[They thrust together, one sword point at the neck of SIMON, another at the neck of RICHARD: both transfixed in terror. JEHAN , the OTHERS flee]

SIMON
Help us! You cowards!

RICHARD
Murder!

[SIMON and RICHARD drop knives, await their fate]

BURIDAN
Orsini!

[ORSINI appears]

These two deserve they should be
hanged.
[To SIMON and RICHARD]
Do you not?

SIMON
Oui.

RICHARD
Oui.

BURIDAN
Stand as sentinels, still, while
Orsini raises the alarm...
[To ORSINI]
You can fetch wine.
[To SIMON & RICHARD]
What say you?

[Exit ORSINI]

SIMON
Nothing. Naught.

RICHARD
Naught. Nothing.

BURIDAN
Very well. I pardon you - present
you your lives intact.

[*His sword comes up*]

    Allez au vice!

[*They flee. Enter ORSINI with wine*]

PHILIPPE
Messire! If ever you are in like
straits you may call on me.

BURIDAN
Messire, your hand?

PHILIPPE
With all my heart!

BURIDAN
    It is enough.

[*They shake hands and BURIDAN toasts*]

    A votre santé mon jeune soldat!

Are you fresh come to Paris?

PHILIPPE
Indeed. But two hours. I came to
see the Queen, her ceremonial entry
and civic welcome.

BURIDAN
Marguerite? She is not yet queen.

PHILIPPE
Oh but will be, tomorrow, the day
after... as soon as Louis is here
from Navarre.

[*He also enters*]

BURIDAN
Where have you served?

PHILIPPE
Flanders.

BURIDAN
They fight well there.

PHILIPPE
They do. Too well.

BURIDAN
I come from Italy.

PHILIPPE
They fight well in Italy.

BURIDAN
Excellently.

PHILIPPE
I seek my fortune.

BURIDAN
I do that.

Your fortunate expectations?

PHILIPPE
My brother captains the Queen's
Guard.

BURIDAN
Ah! Gaultier d'Aulnay.

You are sure of favourite
advancement, your brother is
refused nothing.

PHILIPPE
Yes yes... I am told as much. I
have sent him message I am here.

The rabble gone, shall you honour
me with your name, sir?

BURIDAN
Which name? The name I was born
under or the name I fight under?

PHILIPPE
Which will you give me?

BURIDAN
Buridan. *Nom de guerre.* Earned in
war.

PHILIPPE
I am Philippe d'Aulnay.

BURIDAN
That you are.

PHILIPPE
Have you anyone at court?

BURIDAN
Not one, in the common court.

PHILIPPE
What have you to offer?

BURIDAN
My sword, my head and my heart.

PHILIPPE
You are a fine looking man - you
need rely on nothing else.
[*A laugh*]
Love and admiration languish your
lot!

BURIDAN
Perhaps. You are gentle. But I do
have more.

Like Marguerite I am from Burgundy,
I served her father Duke Robert as
his page before his assassinate
death, we were children, she and I
and... we have a secret.

PHILIPPE
Ah!

BURIDAN
A secret that may lead to my death
or... my fortune.

PHILIPPE
Oh, bonne...

[*Drinking to BURIDAN*]
...oui... bonne chance!

BURIDAN
To you also, *mon soldat!*

PHILIPPE
I have it. I am already fortunate.

I have been approached discreetly,
behalf a young and beautiful lady
who has an... interest in soldiers.
[*Shows the ring*]
At toll of curfew on the corner of
rue Froid-Mantel tonight I am urged
give this ring to a man will ask to see it...

[*VEILED WOMAN appears*]
The same woman!
[*Continues addressing BURIDAN*]
I am then to follow the man...
[*Stopping again*]
It is the same woman, I swear. See
she beckons you.

[*The VEILED WOMAN beckons from the quay. Music*]

VEILED WOMAN
Capitaine?

PHILIPPE
It is her. Shall you go out to
her?

[*BURIDAN picks up his cloak and goes out, followed by PHILIPPE*]

❖

SCENE 3

Quay. The banks of the Seine

[*VEILED WOMAN beckons again to BURIDAN, hisses*]

VEILED WOMAN
Capitaine!

BURIDAN
Ma gracieuse?

[*As PHILIPPE joins BURIDAN the VEILED WOMAN shakes her head, backs away*]

PHILIPPE
She will not speak.

BURIDAN
Why will she not?
[*Shaking his head*]
You will pardon my discretion?

[*BURIDAN leaves PHILIPPE and goes to the VEILED WOMAN, bends to listen while she whispers*]

VEILED WOMAN
A beautiful lady who loves the
sword finds yours to her liking,
she wonders to herself...

[*She drops her voice so that only BURIDAN can hear. He listens some more and then exclaims:*]

BURIDAN
Am I valiant? Am I worthy of trust?
[*Indignantly*]
I have put Italians to the sword
for twenty years - the worst
villains I have ever contended.

My sword has fleshed their women
for a like number of years - they

are the slyest, most lubricious,
lickerous and ruttish it has ever
contented.

You may tell your mistress I never
refuse a challenge, a *rendezvous* or
a combat - all I ask is that my
opponent is belted and spurred, *mia
innamorata*, young and beautiful.

VEILED WOMAN
Elle est jeune, elle est belle.

BURIDAN
Va bene. The ring....?
[*She gives him the ring*]

VEILED WOMAN
Adieu mon capitaine; courage et plaisir!
[*Exit VEILED WOMAN*]

PHILIPPE
A *rendezvous?*

BURIDAN
Si.

PHILIPPE
Where?

BURIDAN
The second tower of the Louvre, its
shadow.

PHILIPPE
A ring?

BURIDAN
Oui.

PHILIPPE
Show me.

BURIDAN
Here.

PHILIPPE
The same. Sorcery. Shall you go?

                    BURIDAN

Oui.

                    PHILIPPE

    Sisters?

                    BURIDAN

Then we become brothers-in-love.

[*PHILIPPE looks off*]

                    PHILIPPE

Chut!

    Here is Gaultier... my only
    brother.

[*Enter GAULTIER D'AULNAY*]

                    GAULTIER

    Philippe. It is I, Gaultier.

                    PHILIPPE

    Brother!

                    GAULTIER

.   Your hand, brother. Yes yes, it is
    really you - at last!

                    PHILIPPE

Oui, c'est moi!

                    GAULTIER

    Is your love for me strong as
    ever?

                    PHILIPPE

    As ever. You are part of me.

                    GAULTIER

    As ever. We are one.

[*They embrace. Then clasping each the other by the
shoulder, grin*]

                    PHILIPPE

    As ever.

                    GAULTIER

    Who is he?

PHILIPPE

A friend of but one hour who came
to my aid with sword and valour.

Some rogues chose to insult you - I
found myself beset ten to one.

[*GAULTIER salutes BURIDAN*]

GAULTIER

Messire! Whatever you ask of
Gaultier d'Aulnay, whatever; bid
him pray at your mother's grave and
God willing he'll be there; bid him
rise up from his knees before his
mistress - then let God guard her
port for he will sail.

At your first call he will come to
you and whether you need him shed
blood or life, he will; as he now
gives his hand.

BURIDAN

Yours is a sacred love, gentlemen.

PHILIPPE

It is. It is all we have in the
world, he, for me; me, for him.

Because we were born twins without
parents, a red cross on our left
arms our only means of recognition.

GAULTIER

Because we were abandoned together
on the cobbles of Notre Dame, *oui*.

PHILIPPE

Because we have starved together,
shivered together we are rekindled,
fulfilled, inspirited by each the
other... *conjointement!*

GAULTIER

When he dies I shall die, and, as
he came into the world a few hours
before I did, I swear I shall live
only those same few hours after his
death... my love, and everything I
have is his...

PHILIPPE

All I own is yours!

GAULTIER

Ours.

Our horse, our purse, our sword on
a signal...

PHILIPPE

Our life on a word!

GAULTIER

Au revoir, capitaine.

To my quarters, Philippe...

PHILIPPE

Ah!

Someone... I am... there is someone
waits for me to attend her... this
night... brother.

GAULTIER

Take care, Philippe.
[*Concerned*]
You are young, you are a stranger.

Take care brother, I would not see
your body brought out the Seine as
young men have been - a curse on
their secret slayer.

PHILIPPE

Captain? You will go?

BURIDAN
I will.

PHILIPPE
I must, I have given my word.

GAULTIER
Our word is sacred, yes.
[*A shrug*]
It's done, given. But tomorrow,
tomorrow morning, when the queen
rises you must attend her court,
brother...?

PHILIPPE
Oui. All is well.

[*GAULTIER worried, turns to BURIDAN, his hand out*]

GAULTIER
Messire, go well.

BURIDAN
Merci.

[*The sound of the curfew. Enter ORSINI. To close his doors, shutters, take down his vine leaves*]

ORSINI
That is the curfew, messeigneurs.

BURIDAN
Adieu! I'm for the Louvre.

[*Exit BURIDAN*]

PHILIPPE
Me, rue Froid-Mantel.

[*Exit PHILIPPE*]

GAULTIER
I have duty at the Palace.

[*Exit GAULTIER*]

[*ORSINI left. The curfew still ringing*]

ORSINI
Me... the Tower of Nesle!
[*Evil laughter*]
[*Exit ORSINI, his laughter becoming diabolical music*]

SCENE 4

Streets of Paris. Night

[*It rains. A young MAN is led through the wet darkness, his eyes bandaged, then another, unmistakable shape of BURIDAN, eyes bandaged, then PHILIPPE, the same. Thunder, lightning, music of laughter*]

SCENE 5

The Tower of Nesle
Night

[*Discovered, ORSINI at a window of the Petit Tower of Nesle*]

ORSINI
Cric! It is the most beautiful
night for an orgy! *Crac!*
[*Closing shutters*]
Cric! The sky is black, rain
tumbles, the city sleeps and our
river swells, laps up for its feed
of corpses... a perfect time for
love; outside, the thump and crack
of thunder; inside - a sibilance of
skin, kisses, whispers, slip of
silk, tink of glass; an outlandish

conjunction of God and Satan - a
sea simmers, little pink fish, in
and out, in and out...

[*Laughter heard from the taller tower*]

Laugh then, young fools.
[*Yawning*]
Me, I wait; you have an hour left
to live- me, an hour left to wait
as I waited last night and tomorrow
and tomorrow and tomorrow. What
nice malignancy! Inexorable fate!

Young eyes have seen what they
should not, lips have sucked where
they should not - sucked and been
sucked, seeing and not seeing.

Cric! Those eyes shall be put out,
those lips sealed until the day
they howl their accusations before
the throne of God! *Crac!*

What misfortune!

Misfortune a hundred times merited
by these imprudent gallants who
prick to the call of a night of
"*l'amour*", are hustled, engorged,
through storm thunder and lashing
flood, their eyes bandaged, their
steps prescribed, simply that they
might utter the words: "*je t'aime*",
to three spoiled women, young,
beautiful, drunk on lust, wine and
their own voluptuousness.

They can never have presumed there
was no price to pay?

Cric! There is... and I wait as a
landlord waits, to exact it. *Crac!*

[*Outside the call of the WATCH is heard:* "Il est deux heures, la pluie tombe, tout est tranquille. Parisiens dormez". *ORSINI shrugs*]

[*Enter LANDRY, the shambling one eyed sergeant, in his footless hose, filthy white coif, disgruntled*]

LANDRY

Mâitre!

ORSINI

Che c'e ora?

LANDRY

It is two in the morning, you heard
the watch?

ORSINI

I did. Day is a long time off.

LANDRY

The others fret...

ORSINI

Zut! They get pay.

LANDRY

If I might be bold, they are paid
to kill not to wait. If they wait
they ought have a double sum - so
much for boredom - so much for
slaughtering.

ORSINI

Hold thy tongue, Landry.

Someone comes. Go! *Muoviti,
cammina!*

LANDRY

I will go, but what you tell me is
without... justice.

[*Exit LANDRY even more disgruntled*]

[*Enter MARGUERITE, imperious, ravishingly beautiful, suffused with passion, deshabille*]

                    MARGUERITE
          Orsini!

                    ORSINI
          Madame!

                    MARGUERITE
          The men?

                    ORSINI
          Ready. Night flees.

                    MARGUERITE
          Is it so late?

                    ORSINI
          The storm drops.

                    MARGUERITE
          Hark! Thunder.

                    ORSINI
          Day beckons.

                    MARGUERITE
          No no, Orsini, it is again
          darkening... oh!

[*A flash of lightning*]

                    ORSINI
          Madame, the lights must be doused,
          cushions, beds... your boat waits
          to take you home and we are left
          our work as usual...

                    MARGUERITE
          But it is not as usual, this night,
          this young man is not and the night
          is not.

          He is like to another, above all
          others, do you not see it, Orsini?

ORSINI
Like to who?

MARGUERITE
Gaultier d'Aulnay. As I look up at
him, listen to him, I see Gaultier,
hear my Gaultier.

This is a boy all full of love and
passion.

What danger can he be to me or to
you, this child?

ORSINI
A plaything - not a child - to be
taken and then dashed to pieces as
the others have been.

This boy, the more you did enjoy
his bawls - the more you have to
fear.
[*Urgently*]
It is nigh three o'clock. Leave him.

MARGUERITE:
No, he's mine. Others may do as
they please. This young man is mine
to save.

I never dropped my mask. Should he
see me tomorrow he would not know
my face.

He must be returned to the city
safely, sound. See to it, Orsini.

I grant it. So be it. He will live
to remember this night, burn with
the memory, heavenly dreams of love
which come but once to us on this
earth, for him, and I wish, for me.

ORSINI
Signora.

MARGUERITE
Oui. Save him. Put up your knives,
open the doors, but hurry...

[*Exit ORSINI*]

[*PHILIPPE is heard off:* "My love, my life, my angel,
what is your name?" *MARGUERITE puts her mask back
on. Enter PHILIPPE*]

PHILIPPE
I must call you by your name!

MARGUERITE
It is day.

PHILIPPE
Day, night is of no matter, torches
flare, wine sparkles, hearts beat
and time passes. Come again, again.

MARGUERITE
No no, no more... we must part.

PHILIPPE
Part! I may never see you again.
That would be despair. We belong
one to the other! Part the links
of a chain and it is in pieces.

MARGUERITE
You promised me you would resign
to parting... it is time, my husband
will wake and look for me... it is
already light.

PHILIPPE
No no, that is the moon's light, it
slips through the clouds as I slip,
we slip... again, again.

Your husband sleeps the sleep of
the old, close to death the closer
to the day.

Again, again, an hour, then *adieu!*

MARGUERITE
No! Not an hour, not an instant. I
beg you... go!

At once, without a backward glance,
never to say a word to anyone, not
even your dearest friend...

Go, from Paris, from me, now. *Now!*

PHILIPPE
Eh bien.
Oui. But... your name? Tell me.
It will sound in my ears eternal,
it will be written on my heart.

Your name? I wish to sing it ever
coming in my dreams - I know you to
be noble, beautiful and divine!

Oh, give me your colours, that I
might bear them on my lance?

I came to you at your wish but I
have looked for you for ever!

Cry your name and kiss me gone, let
me die, your favour on my helm.

MARGUERITE
Non. The night is over, all is done
and you are free, as I am free.

We are not bound to each other, not
you to me or I to you. Obey me if
you love me, obey me if you do not.
[*Coldly*] I am a woman, in my house. I order
you from me, out of it. Go!

PHILIPPE
I petition and you scoff, I plead
and you whip me from you.
Very well, I shall go. *Adieu.*

MARGUERITE
Oui!

[*To her gasp of relief, PHILIPPE turns to go and then plucking a pin from her coif, scratches her cheek*]

PHILIPPE
Now I shall know you!

MARGUERITE
Oh!

PHILIPPE
Keep your name in your breast.

This bloody badge on your cheek
will tell me, next we meet, you,
are... my love!

MARGUERITE
Oh you fool.
[*Wearily aside*]
He has wound me and killed himself.

[*Exit MARGUERITE to shriek of eldritch music. The light goes with her. PHILIPPE left alone in the darkness. Doors slam throughout the Towers. Feet scurry up stone steps, a scuffle and a cry. PHILIPPE gasps in fear as a hand touches his shoulder*]

PHILIPPE
Qui est la!

BURIDAN
Moi.

PHILIPPE
Buridan!

BURIDAN
Oui. Do you know where we are?

PHILIPPE
No.

BURIDAN
Non. Aaaaagh, these ripe women.

[*Spits - wipes*]
Do you know who they are?

PHILIPPE
No, I have no name, I saw no face.

BURIDAN
No, you did not... no...

PHILIPPE
What is it excites you, you tremble
with fear, no not fear, rage...?

BURIDAN
Anger, such anger. These women are
the highest in the land, you saw,
you felt that, hands pale and soft.

Have you felt before such hands on
your body - not the chap and chafe
and jerking hands of siege sluts,
garrison whores - such cold smile?

What rich clothes they shed to take
us in - her voice so soft enticing,
eyes such guile.

We are brought in the night by an
old veiled woman who drips sweet
words... noble ladies, she tells
us they are noble ladies!

Oh they *are* noble ladies!

Brought a'stumble, wet, blinded - a
dazzling place, the perfume stench
and warmth is heady - they embrace
us and with a thousand tender
caresses, give themselves without
restraint or delay, at once...

At once, open!

Open... to strangers, draggled,
dirty, drenched wet from the storm.

Yet they are the noblest of women!

At table - and we both know this to
be true - at table, they are
shameless, oblivious to everything
that is not lust or gratification.

Carried away by fumes of wine, the
rank liquor of concupiscence they
scream blasphemies, hold strange
obscene discourse, utter disgusting
words, forget all propriety, all
decency, forget the world, forget
the sky...!

For they are great and noble women
they are the highest in the land,
they are - *grandes dames tres grandes dames!*
[*Bitterly*]
Ca ira! It goes on.

PHILIPPE

So?

BURIDAN

So? Are you not afraid?

PHILIPPE

Afraid yes, but of what...?

BURIDAN

The care they take to hide their
discovering.

PHILIPPE

What care? I shall know mine do I
see her tomorrow.

BURIDAN

You saw her?

PHILIPPE

No, but with this gold pin from her
coif I cut her face.

BURIDAN
Now we are dead.

PHILIPPE
What?

[*BURIDAN shoves him to the window. Through the shutter crack*]

BURIDAN
There, what do you see?

PHILIPPE
The Louvre.

BURIDAN
There, below, what swirls?

PHILIPPE
The Seine.

BURIDAN
The walls which keep us are of the
Tower of Nesle.

PHILIPPE
The Tower of Nesle!

BURIDAN
Under which so many corpses are
found.

PHILIPPE
And we are unmanned!
Did you slack your sword? They
disarmed me of mine.

BURIDAN
Of what use swords now? Our only
hope is flight. The door...?

[*PHILIPPE tries it, kicks with his foot*]

PHILIPPE
Shut tight.

Mon Dieu. Hear me... my friend, if
I am slain you must take revenge.

BURIDAN
I swear it, and if I am killed, you
must avenge my mortal fate.

PHILIPPE
I swear it.

BURIDAN
Your brother Gaultier, he has
power, to him, tell him that you
seek to avenge me. I will do the
same, you dead, but from me he will
demand proof... write it...

PHILIPPE
No pen, no ink, no parchment.

BURIDAN
We must write it!

Here in this my order tablet, you
have the pin, you have veins, write
in blood, write now, write: "I was
killed by... "

I will uncover her, I will post her
name... she is of the court...

[*PHILIPPE writes in blood:* "I was killed by.."]

We must flee from here our separate
ways, the better we might escape.

PHILIPPE
I from where I came, the other
tower -I will avenge you, Buridan.

BURIDAN
Very well, Philippe.

[*He takes the pin*]

PHILIPPE
Adieu.

BURIDAN

Adieu. In life and death *we* are
one.

[*They embrace*]

[*Exit PHILIPPE up the tall tower steps*]

[*BURIDAN tugs at door, then at the shutters of the window.
Back to the door which is thrust open by LANDRY*]

LANDRY

Say some prayers, young man.

BURIDAN

I know that pikeman voice. Landry!

LANDRY

Buridan! Captain...?

[*A shout. Then blood curdling cries:* "Murder! Murder!"]

BURIDAN

Landry. For the love of heaven save
me - we have fought together.

They seek to kill me also.

LANDRY

I am sent to.

BURIDAN

Who is that? Who cries "Murder!"

LANDRY

They are cutting his throat.

BURIDAN

The staircase?

LANDRY

Leads nowhere...

BURIDAN

The window?

LANDRY

Can you swim?

BURIDAN

Yes.

LANDRY

There is no other way...
[*Tugging open the shutters*]
Dieu vous garde, capitaine!

BURIDAN

[*Looks down, hastily crosses himself*]
"Dieu, ayez pitie de moi!"

[*He leaps from the window. Splash heard*]

[*Enter ORSINI. He has heard the splash, asks of LANDRY:*]

ORSINI

Oui?

LANDRY

Dead. In the river.

[*A crash and a stumble*]

[*Enter PHILIPPE backwards into the room from the stair-case, blood streaming from wounds in his chest*]

[*Enter MARGUERITE pursuing him. In her hand a bloody knife. PHILIPPE turns, down on his knees*]

PHILIPPE

Au secours! Au secours. Mon
frère! a moi, mon frère!

MARGUERITE

Look then, and die!

[*Standing behind him she removes her mask, tugs his head round so that he might see her face. He gasps:*]

PHILIPPE

Marguerite, Queen of France!

[*She cuts his throat and he dies*]

❖

SCENE 6

Private apartments of the
Queen in the Louvre
Day

[*MARGUERITE is asleep on her bed. The sound of birds, shafts of sunlight through curtains. She lies in sumptuousness*]

[*Music*]

[*Enter GAULTIER through a secret door. He approaches the bed, on tip-toe, sits at the head, asks softly:*]

GAULTIER
Have the angels of heaven given you
peace as you sleep, golden dreams,
my queen? Have they my thanks?

[*MARGUERITE still in daze of slumber, smiles, her eyes still closed, stretches*]

MARGUERITE
I have slept and I have seen in my
sleep a young man very like you,
Gaultier, your eyes, your voice,
your delicacies of love...
[*She sits up*]
...but, I felt pain... here.

GAULTIER
You have a scratch on your cheek.

MARGUERITE
Yes, I feel it.
[*Aside*]
Oh! je me rapelle...
[*To him*]

I remember, a pin from my coif
rolled down the pillow... aaah!

[*GAULTIER touches her cheek gently*]

GAULTIER
Let me see... yes... take care of
your beauty Marguerite, it is not
just yours, it is mine as well...

MARGUERITE
It was not you in my dream, it was
your shadow, your mirroring.

GAULTIER
Then it was my brother spoke to
you, my other person, half my life,
my very second... love.

MARGUERITE
And the first...?

GAULTIER
You. You are hope, life, existence,
I live through you. I count the
beat of my heart in the beat of
yours, a touch is enough. Could I
but enter your body as you live in
mine... kiss your soul...?

MARGUERITE
No sweet friend, my dear, no, let
me have your pure love, for a queen
lives in fear of indiscretion, one
sneer is enough to bring her death.

Suffocate between two rude pallets
will be my fate, but you... he will
castrate.

Take heart that I love you as you
love me and never fail to say you
do... words of love like music.

GAULTIER
Tomorrow he comes, the music dies.

MARGUERITE
Your king. He comes to claim his
throne - farewell trysts, farewell
long sweet meanderings, farewell
liberty - he comes to claim his
city, his crown, his land and me.

Can you still see the scar?

GAULTIER

Yes.

[*Fanfare. Noise*]

MARGUERITE

So late!

GAULTIER
Yes, you must dress...

[*He starts to go, an order tablet drops from his sleeve*]

MARGUERITE
Pick it up, go... no, let me see...

[*She reaches for it. He laughs, holds it from her, above her
as she reaches*]

GAULTIER

No no...

MARGUERITE
Yes, let me see it... what is it?

GAULTIER
An order tablet, give me at my duty

post this morning by a Franciscan,
it comes from a man I met with my
brother.
[*Holds it from her*]
Philippe, shall you receive him?

MARGUERITE
Your brother? Present him this
morning.
[*Reaching again*]
Let me see... is it poems, essays
of love?

[*GAULTIER evades her, still laughing, slipping the book
into his sleeve again*]

GAULTIER
No, not, I know not for I am sworn
on Christ's cross by the holy old
man not to open it for two days.
[*He shrugs*]
My brother's friend, mine become,
fears misfortune.
[*Smiles*]
Should it happen to him, I am sworn
I must open it. I must go.

MARGUERITE
I shall see it.

GAULTIER
The court hastens to your rising. I
must be seen impatient, with them.

MARGUERITE
Yes yes, but not of them for you
are my lord, my real lord, my true
master, my king, for who else
reigns if love rules? *Au revoir.*

GAULTIER
Yet...?

MARGUERITE
Go! You must...

[*She draws the last curtain of her bed, but thrusts out her
hand as she calls:* "Charlotte! Charlotte!"]

[*GAULTIER kisses her hand and exits through secret door*]
[*Enter CHARLOTTE*]

CHARLOTTE
Madame?

[*MARGUERITE gestures with her hand then withdraws it*]

MARGUERITE
Faites ouvrir les appartements.

CHARLOTTE
Faites ouvrir les appartements!

[*The call goes up throughout the palace. Trumpets, drums*]

SCENE 7

The corridors of the Palace
Day

[*CHAMBERLAINS, GUARDS, ATTENDANTS open drapes, curtains, doors, shutters and sunlight streams in. They call:* "Faites ouvrir les appartements! La Reine! La Reine!"]

[*Enter COURTIERS, PIERREFONDS, SAVOISY, RAOUL then GAULTIER. They form their groups of interest - chaperon hats, wide sleeved garnache cloaks of splendid silks, velvets*]

SAVOISY
Ah, Gaultier, you got here betimes.
As ever.

GAULTIER
No no...

SAVOISY
How does the Queen rise?
[*Declaiming*]

How does Marguerite, of France,
Burgundy and of Navarre rise,
this sun-blest day?

GAULTIER
Messire, how can I know?

Salut, messieurs, *salut!*

Does my brother ask for me? What
news of the night?

SAVOISY
The King sends flags, heralds, will
enter the city tomorrow and Messire
de Marigny orders the people must
cry: "*Noel!*" along the route...
Until then, they cry: "*Malediction*"
along the banks of the Seine.

GAULTIER
Why?

SAVOISY
Another young man dead, one wearies
of fishing them out.

DE PIERREFONDS
They damn de Marigny for it. So
they should. He is give charge of
our safety. He vaunts his power.
[*Dropping his voice*]
The more corpses the better if we
can bury him under them.

GAULTIER
[*To another group of COURTIERS*]
I expect my brother, messieurs...

DE PIERREFONDS
Should the King not take care he
will lose a good third of his
noblest and richest subjects, all
of them fine young men I am told.

But what possesses them to choose
drowning? To go off so, like they
are kittens or worth no thought?

SAVOISY
Seigneur, surely you do not believe
they take particular care to float
dorsum, weed choked, in the Seine?

DE PIERREFONDS
Are they led to it by demons, Jack
o'Lanterns?

SAVOISY
Rivers are not most secret places
for bodies to lie - a watery grave
is soon sunk but sooner seen. Water
floats up what the earth eats.

There are many houses from Saint
Paul to the Louvre bathe their feet
in the Seine, open their windows to
the ooze...

RAOUL
The Tower of Nesle.

SAVOISY
Oui. I passed it at two o'clock
this morning, ablaze with light.
I loathe that great black double
thrust of stone which sprouts at
night into a malevolent spirit,
tumescent over the city. Fire
flares from it like from the black
lungs of Hell; black it thrusts,
silent black, under black sky, the
river boiling at its feet...

There are revolting stories.

GAULTIER
Seigneur, you talk of a royal
residence!

[*Enter DE MARIGNY*]

SAVOISY

I do. Enough. The King rides in
tomorrow, and the King, as you all
know cares naught for news of any
body but his own.
[*Seeing DE MARIGNY*]
Is that not so... monsigneur de
Marigny?

DE MARIGNY

Messieurs, first tell me what you
said - that I might give proper
patience to your question.

SAVOISY

We applauded that the people of
Paris were a people most happy to
have Louis the Tenth for king and
in ecstasy to have you monsieur de
Marigny for first minister of the
Treasury... what condign bliss!

DE MARIGNY

They would not fare half so well
did they have you first anything,
monsieur de Savoisy!

[*A shout off:* "La reine, messeigneurs!" *taken up
by GAULTIER*]

GAULTIER

La reine, messeigneurs.

[*Enter MARGUERITE*]

MARGUERITE

Dieu vous garde, messieurs.

❖

SCENE 8

The Queens Morning Progress

[*She walks, with her GUARD and LORDS, through the corridors and audience chambers of the palace, the court-yards, the gardens. Way cleared by GUARDS, swept by courtesy, salutes and curtsies of LADIES and GENTLEMEN of the Court*]

[*Fanfares. Anthems*]

MARGUERITE
Ask what you will of me - what
favour, what justice - for tomorrow
I give way to Louis, my lord, my
master, the King.

[*She talks on the move rarely pausing, attended by CHAR-LOTTE. The PETITIONERS follow, some prostrate themselves, are ignored*]

SAVOISY
Not so, madame!

You remain our Queen, by blood, by
beauty a true ruler of France; as
long as our King, God protect him,
has eyes and a heart.

MARGUERITE
Bravo! vous me flattez, compte.

[*The tight group round her consists of SAVOISY, PIERRE-FONDS, DE MARIGNY, GAULTIER, RAOUL*]

Seigneur Gaultier, where hide you
your brother that he might put de
Savoisy's blandishments to shame?

GAULTIER
I confess to anxiety, madame. He is
not here, though I had his word...

[*They pass a NECROMANCER once, then again. NECRO-MANCER looks hard at CHARLOTTE, her face*]

[*Music. PIERREFONDS regards him aghast*]

DE PIERREFONDS
The necromancer, see him?

SAVOISY
Oui. Is he brought by de Marigny
that he might the better cast his
spell on us?

DE PIERREFONDS
See how he looks at the ladies, at
each face as if to burn brands on
them with his eyes.

Paris seethes with sorcery, every
step one takes may be the last for
gypsies, witches, necromancers,
their curses and their magic - what
else is it brings young men to an
drowned death?

GAULTIER
It is sad truth - another body this
morning below the Tower of Nesle.

DE MARIGNY
Two.

MARGUERITE
[*Aside*] Two?

DE PIERREFONDS
They need blood for their witchery.

SAVOISY
Not water?

DE MARIGNY
It is evil work of more substance
than fetid conjurings.

MARGUERITE
Monsieur de Marigny who would have
us all bewitched by him the better
to order our ways, does not believe

in necromancy, he tells us our fate
and how he will tax for it.

SAVOISY
Throttle for it, at end of his

magisterial rope for it, tried,
taxed and dangled taut. Wizardry.

DE PIERREFONDS
What else can be cause except it is
gypsies, witches and necromancers?

There is one there...

[*Turns - points*] Gone, he's gone!

MARGUERITE
Summon him back, that he might tell
us future things, such as what the
King may announce to monsieur de Marigny
tomorrow. Have him fetched.

[*Exit SAVOISY to look for NECROMANCER. His shout
heard off:* "Come here, gypsy, the Queen needs good
news!"]

DE PIERREFONDS
That they need blood is true, foul
secrets only yield to disgusting
profanities.

[*Enter SAVOISY, bemused, he laughs, shrugs*]

SAVOISY
He comes, but where he went when
coming I know not...

DE PIERREFONDS
Aaaah! His science is give him by
either God or Satan - we do well to
protect ourselves.

[*He makes sign of cross, all except DE MARIGNY join him*]

SCENE 9

The Throne Room
Day

[*The NECROMANCER appears, unseen by all but DE MARIGNY who goes aside to him*]

> DE MARIGNY
> Sorcerer, if you wish a welcome in
> this company proclaim a thousand
> scandals rather than merely one, a
> thousand deaths, not one, and know
> that however you may excite the
> others I shall hear you calmly and
> with complete disbelief - now spin.

> NECROMANCER
> Make your atonement with God. You
> have three more days of life.

[*SAVOISY exclaims in laughter, seeing him:*]

> SAVOISY
> He passeth through walls!

> DE MARIGNY
> I thank you - there are none know
> with certainty they have... three
> hours to live.

[*The NECROMANCER sweeps his arm, points, resting on GAULTIER, SAVOISY reacting in mock horror as the finger passes over*]

> NECROMANCER
> You sir? You are Gaultier d'Aulnay
> and you wait your brother but... he
> does not come.

> GAULTIER
> Where is he?

NECROMANCER
They throng the banks of the Seine.

GAULTIER
My brother!

NECROMANCER
They surround two bodies and cry
out "*Malediction!*"

GAULTIER
My brother!

NECROMANCER
One. Go down to the river.

GAULTIER
My brother!

NECROMANCER
See the left arm of one of the
drowned then cry: "*Malediction!*"

GAULTIER
My brother! My brother!

[*Exit GAULTIER precipitantly. SAVOISY comments
drily:*]

SAVOISY
Lo! He sees what others have seen
but as they passeth not through
walls have not come yet to tell us.

[*COURTIERS follow to watch GAULTIER go. MARGUE-
RITE standing motionless, the smile of dismissal fixed on
her face and becomes a grimace, the finger of the NECRO-
MANCER pointing at her, pale, her cheek with its red
scratch towards him. He says quietly:*]

NECROMANCER
Marguerite de Bourgogne!

Is royal destiny beyond divination.
Can mere mortal not see, not read?

[*COURTIERS turn back, their laughter freezing at sight of the QUEEN, her pale anger and fear. They mutter:* "The Queen! Is she witched?" *The mood has changed to discomfiture*]

MARGUERITE
I wish to know nothing, nothing.

[*DE MARIGNY at her side, hand on sword, solid, dependable and MARGUERITE clutches at him, then flees to her throne as if for sanctuary*]

NECROMANCER
And yet you would have me come, me
here, Marguerite... you must now
heed what I tell you.

MARGUERITE
Do not withdraw, monsieur de
Marigny.
[*Her hand out to DE MARIGNY again*]

NECROMANCER
Oh Marguerite! Marguerite! why
must your nights be darkest black
without... warm bright within?

MARGUERITE
Who fetched this gypsy? Who asked
for him? What does he want of me?

[*NECROMANCER has reached the throne, foot on the steps*]

NECROMANCER
Marguerite, is there not, by your
count, one body less? Did you not
believe, this morning, there would
be three bodies and not two?

MARGUERITE
Say no more, unless it is what
gives you this power of divination.

NECROMANCER
Here is my talisman, Marguerite.
[*The pin*]
Ah! Your hand flies to your cheek.
[*Aside*] It is she!
[*Aloud*] Very well, I have more to say, but
to you alone, madame.
[*To DE MARIGNY*]
Leave us, seigneur de Marigny.

DE MARIGNY
I shall not. I take orders from
none but the queen...

MARGUERITE
Then take them, and go.
[*To the COURT*]
Go! Leave! Go!

[*Leaving DE MARIGNY, MARGUERITE comes down from
the throne, takes the NECROMANCER aside, he whispers
urgently:*]

NECROMANCER
Your love, your honour, your very
life is in my hands.

MARGUERITE
Yes yes...

NECROMANCER
At curfew tonight I shall wait for
you at Orsini's tavern.

MARGUERITE
No, a Queen of France cannot...

NECROMANCER
It is no distance, it wants but a
bolt flight from...
[*Raising his voice*]
...the Tower of Nesle.

MARGUERITE
I shall come, I shall come.

NECROMANCER
Bring parchment and the Seal.

MARGUERITE
I will. So be it.

NECROMANCER
Go back, shut up your apartments to
all.

MARGUERITE
To all?

NECROMANCER
Most above all, Gaultier d'Aulnay.
[*Going*]
Messeigneurs, the Queen commends
you to God!
[*To MARGUERITE*]
A ce soir, chez Orsini, Marguerite.

MARGUERITE
A ce soir.

[*Exit MARGUERITE in haste. Shouts. Doors close throughout the palace:* "Fermez les appartements!" "Fermez...!"]

[*Exit the NECROMANCER/BURIDAN, the COURTIERS reeling back from him as he goes*]

DE PIERREFONDS
Is this man not Satan, himself?

SAVOISY
Monsieur de Marigny?

DE PIERREFONDS
What was said?

SAVOISY
Monsieur?

DE MARIGNY
I heard, messieurs but I remember
only that which concerns me.

SAVOISY
Oui?

DE PIERREFONDS
Will you not henceforth take heed?

DE MARIGNY
Why now, when I would not before?
He predicted disgrace, I am still
in office; he predicts my death
and, by the living God, messieurs,
if you need assurance that I am
alive and well, say so, I have a
sword will speak for me!

[*A cry off:* "Justice!"]

[*Enter GAULTIER, distraught*]

GAULTIER
Justice! My brother, messeigneurs,
my brother Philippe, my only
friend, my only kinsman, throat
cut, drowned, dragged up on the
banks of that accursed river... I
demand justice, I demand his killer
that I may chew from him his neck,
set my feet on his foul carcase...

[*Accusing DE MARIGNY*]

You, messire, you must answer to me
for this! On you it sits! You
guard our city, noble blood shed is
blood smeared on your honour...

SAVOISY
Gaultier, my friend...

[*GAULTIER throws himself at the doors to the QUEEN's apartments*]

GAULTIER

I have no friend. I had a brother I
have no more, I must have him live
or his murderer dead. Marguerite!

[*Hammering on the doors*]

Marguerite!

[*GUARDS and DE MARIGNY pull him from the doors. He
draws his sword. A half circle of GUARDS, DE MARIGNY,
SAVOISY around him, their swords drawn*]

DE MARIGNY

Stand, hold, young man!

SAVOISY

Gaultier!

[*GAULTIER launches himself at them. DE MARIGNY
defends the doors from his frenzied assault, the GUARDS
reel back, one injured, SAVOISY scratches GAULTIER at
the shoulder, another GUARD beats down his sword and
GAULTIER sobs:*]

GAULTIER

I demand justice of the Queen!

[*Exit GAULTIER, bloody and distraught*]

SCENE 10

Streets. River. Gate Saint Honore
Night

[*Toll of Curfew. MARGUERITE, veiled, cloaked against
night. Recognition sweeps through the emptying streets
and miasma of the river towards the Gate of Saint-Honore.
Music. Behind her, unseen by her, follows GAULTIER.
Loud knocking*]

SCENE 11

Orsini's Tavern
Night

[*A small dark smoke filled room, with fire, some furniture but not much, rushes on the floor.*]

[*Enter ORSINI. Bowing low*]

ORSINI
House and master, signora, command
me and mine.

[*Enter MARGUERITE uncovering her face*]

MARGUERITE
I want nothing but your quittance.

ORSINI
Signora, I am gone.

MARGUERITE
Stay.
[*Listens*] I am alone and at this hour.

ORSINI
Alone and at this hour.

MARGUERITE
Which is strange.
[*Listens*]
That which makes me come alone and
at this hour is strange...

[*A knock*]
...also. A knock?

ORSINI
A knock. That door.
[*He points*]

MARGUERITE
I shall open it. Your quittance.

ORSINI

I am gone. *Volatilizzarsi!*

MARGUERITE

Silent, on your life.

ORSINI

I am deaf, I am without a tongue
but if you need me I shall hear.

[*Another knock*]

MARGUERITE

I will attend it.

[*Exit ORSINI*]

BURIDAN

[*Speaking off*]
Open the door, Marguerite.

MARGUERITE

Is it you, necromancer?

BURIDAN

It is.

[*MARGUERITE opens the door and recoils in fear. Enter
BURIDAN, in half mail, leather jerkin, sword and dagger,
a red painted sallet*]

MARGUERITE

You are not the gypsy...?

BURIDAN

No, by God, I am Christian, was,
have been, faith only lives with
hope, I have been without both.

[*He sits MARGUERITE says coldly through her fear*]

MARGUERITE

I expect you to uncover and stand.

BURIDAN

I shall do so.

[*Stands - removes sallet*]

Not for you are a queen, but that
you are a woman. There is no queen
here, see these smoked walls, this
floor, its straw... is there here
any trinket, asset, chattel of a
queen?

Queen, where are your guards? See,
where is your throne?

Here is a woman trembles hot and
pallid in anger and fear and a man
is cold as ice.

I am crowned king for my demeanor.

                MARGUERITE
Who are you?

                BURIDAN
You know my name which was.

                MARGUERITE
I do not.

                BURIDAN
Now it is Buridan.

                MARGUERITE
I know it not.

                BURIDAN
You are afraid. Your guards drag
chains in the Seine - for what do
they look?

They look for another body.

They look for me.

                MARGUERITE
C'est impossible!
                BURIDAN
Impossible?

In the Tower of Nesle were three
noble ladies, their names the
highest in the land, the princess
Jeanne, the princess Blanche, and
the queen, Marguerite.

With them were Hector de Chevreuse,
Philippe d'Aulnay, and Buridan the
captain from Burgundy. Me.

MARGUERITE

Burgundy?

BURIDAN

Oui, Burgundy.

MARGUERITE

They are dead, you live.

BURIDAN

I live. Gaultier d'Aulnay lives, swears to
avenge his brother. He the one who
scratched your cheek.

MARGUERITE

The queen loves Gaultier d'Aulnay,
he her.

[*Scorn*] You will speak to Gaultier d'Aulnay
and tell him that the queen killed
his brother?

You are a fool Buridan. You will
not be believed.

Now that I have your secret as you
have mine it needs only a sign from
me for you, Buridan, captain, from
Burgundy to be poled down where you
stand.

BURIDAN

It needs more.

It needs a notes book and what is
writ within it, in blood, which

blood there was plenty before you
opened his neck.

Gaultier d'Aulnay has the last
blood writ words of his brother and
he is sworn fast, by a priest of
St Francis he will read them should
I not stand before him, tomorrow at
ten o'clock.

I, Buridan, captain, who saw
scratched in fear and rage, "I was
killed by Marguerite de Bourgogne"...
with a gold pin, from your coif.

This pin.

There is as well a second secret.

Marguerite, anatomise, dig into my
heart with twenty poignards and you
will not exhume this second secret.
Have me slid into the Seine to
embrace again the shades of my
companions of the night, Philippe,
poor shrieking Hector, my secret
will float upon the surface and
tomorrow at stroke of ten,
Gaultier, my avenger, will cry out
for an accounting, demand blood
price for his brother and for
me."I shall come from the knees
of my mistress", he said, in oath
to me! Am I a fool?

                    MARGUERITE
If this is so.

                    BURIDAN
It is so.

                    MARGUERITE
What will I give you... let you
plunge your hands into my treasure

for gold, the specie of the state;
or the death of an enemy perhaps?
[*The seal*]

Here is the Seal, parchment, you
said I had to bring... are you
ambitious? I can give you whatever
chain of State you wish...

Speak. What?

BURIDAN

All, and more.

Listen to my words Marguerite.
Here we stand, not king or queen
you and I but man and woman bound
by pact we cannot sunder but by
death of one or other - on pain of
malison.

MARGUERITE

What? Speak.

BURIDAN

Marguerite, I want sufficient gold
to pave a palace.

MARGUERITE

You shall have it. I shall melt
down sceptre and crown that you do.

BURIDAN

I would be first minister.

MARGUERITE

De Marigny is that.

BURIDAN

I want his title and place.

MARGUERITE

Not but by his death.

BURIDAN

I want his title and place.

MARGUERITE

You shall.

BURIDAN

You are left your lover and your
secret.

We two will reign, the State and
France ours to dispose.

We two stand one, king and true
king and, I guard my lips for ever.

You shall have a boat, moored each
night, on the river. Those windows
of the palace look out on the Tower
of Nesle will be blinded.

Acceptes-tu, Marguerite?

MARGUERITE

J'accepte.

BURIDAN

You accept that tomorrow at this
hour I shall be first minister of
the Treasury?

MARGUERITE

You will be.

BURIDAN

Tomorrow at ten I shall come to the
court for the little book, my order
tablet, with which I have sent men
their glory.

MARGUERITE

You will be received.

BURIDAN

Now, write an arrest for de
Marigny.

*[MARGUERITE writes and signs the order for DE
MARIGNY's arrest, affixing the Seal]*

MARGUERITE
Here.

[*BURIDAN takes the parchment*]

BURIDAN
*C'est bien, adieu Marguerite, à
demain!*

[*Exit BURIDAN*]

MARGUERITE
[*Spits her rage*]
"*A demain, démon!*"

Fiend! Devil!

God will need help you if the day
comes I have you in my hands as you
have me this night!

[*Going*] Foul, foul fortune follow you who
dare defy me.

Me, a great duke's daughter!

Me, the wife of a king!

Me, me, me, regent of France!

[*Exit MARGUERITE into the night. Music*]

SCENE 12

*The banks of the Seine at
Saint-Honore
Night*

[*MARGUERITE hurrying back to the Louvre, stops and
rages yet again:*]

MARGUERITE
That cursed book! I offer half my
blood to he who brings it me.

GAULTIER [*Off*]
Marguerite!

[*Enter GAULTIER*]

GAULTIER
Marguerite, *c'est toi?*

MARGUERITE
Gaultier!
[*Aside*]
He is come to me.
[*Turning on him*]
Faithless wretch... what do you
here?

GAULTIER
[*Taken aback at her apparent anger*]
I followed you. I seek justice.

MARGUERITE
Justice? Ask me for justice? Give
me that book hides your guilt.

GAULTIER
I have no guilt. I would find my
brother's guilty murderer.

MARGUERITE
Your brother dead will be avenged,
his slayer found - I swear it. Now
give me that which is close to your
heart, some other love confided.

GAULTIER
I have no other love.

MARGUERITE
Then you have no justice given you.

GAULTIER
Marguerite, I must have justice.

MARGUERITE
Must? There is no justice except
of the crown and that not easily
bought - except, in that love may
sway. Give me the book, see justice
flower, on kisses - who loves?

GAULTIER
None but you.

MARGUERITE
You lie.

GAULTIER
You are the repository of all my
love, all I have left now, more,
for my brother gone... there is
more.

MARGUERITE
You lie. Let me feel your heart,
what beat it makes can prove your
innocence or no... justice there.

[*She leans against him. Feels his breast*]

GAULTIER
What do I lie?

MARGUERITE
Your loves. You have a book I'm told, some
words, some songs, a *juec d'amor*,
you are a troubador and ladies of
the court have heard you sing from
it, their names within of it...

GAULTIER
They lie, they lie... I have no
skills of love song, none...

MARGUERITE
You have and here is proof.

[*She plucks the notebook from his sleeve*]

GAULTIER
Oh no! I am sworn, you must not
have it.

MARGUERITE
What are you sworn?
[*Scorn*] What am I sworn? Have I never
broke oath for you? Forget I am
forsworn for you, for treachery in
love is more than in the
adulteress, forget and keep your
word...
[*Giving him back the notebook*]
...and, me, I keep my jealousy.

Justice done, forgot. *Adieu!*

GAULTIER
Marguerite, in heaven's name, keep
me my honour!

MARGUERITE
Honour! The honour of a man!

The honour of a woman, is that then
nothing? You have sworn?

But, me; one word, one thought of
you and I have forgot my oath made
before God.

And I would forget it again, and
again and again, and did you pray
me do so, I would forget the entire
world for you!

[*He holds out to her the notebook*]

GAULTIER
Mon Dieu, pardonnez-moi!
[*Not letting go*]

Is it angels or demons urge me
forget my brother, my oath, my
honour...?

[*He gives it her in agony of indecision. She takes it and
walks from him, saying calmly, aside:*]

MARGUERITE

I have it.

GAULTIER

Forgive me, my brother. I fear that
I, though I know not how, forswear
thee this night.

[*MARGUERITE surreptitiously tears a page from the book
and comes back to GAULTIER, to give it him*]

MARGUERITE

It was a madness. There is nothing
in the book.

My Gaultier does not lie.

[*They embrace*]

You shall have your justice.

The name of your brother's murderer
is known to me.

GAULTIER

His name?

MARGUERITE

He comes to court tomorrow where
you will arrest him.

GAULTIER

His damned name?

MARGUERITE

Precede me to the palace where an
order will be put out for his
arrest, and you shall yourself
arrest him... take care you will?

[*She leads him off, then lets him precede her*]

GAULTIER
I shall, I shall! *Merci, merci, ma
reine...*
[*Going · off*] ...his name?

[*MARGUERITE with the small piece of paper, loiters to say
aside:*]

MARGUERITE
Oh! Buridan, it is now me holds
your life in my hands!

[*Exit MARGUERITE*]

[*The rain starts to fall. Music. The WATCH is heard:* "Il
est deux heures, la pluie tombe, tout est tranquille.
Parisiens dormez"]

SCENE 13

At front of the Louvre

[*Bright morning, bird song. Music*]

[*Discovered RICHARD, looking at the river. Gates of the
Louvre closed. An ARBALÉTRIER in his pepperpot in a
corner of the wall. A balcony*]

[*Enter SIMON. He joins RICHARD and looks up at the
ARBALÉTRIER and contemplates the river with
RICHARD*]

SIMON
C'est toi, Richard?

RICHARD
Oui, c'est moi, Simon.

[*They contemplate the river some more*]

SIMON
You fish?

RICHARD

Non.
[*Another sigh*]
I look for them.

SIMON

Fish?

RICHARD

They go to the devil the highest in
the land and, by water, rather than
by land.

SIMON

Oui. And what do you do here, nose
in the water, back to the palace?

RICHARD

I watch the foot of the Tower of
Nesle for any noble fish on his way
to the devil with his throat cut,
that I might offer him *bon voyage.*

SIMON

None?

RICHARD

None.

[*Another sigh. SIMON then brightens, asks:*]

SIMON

Are they all gone?

RICHARD

Oui!

[*Enter SAVOISY*]

[*RICHARD turning to go comes face to face with him*]

SAVOISY

Get into the gutter, idiot!

RICHARD

Oui, monseigneur...

[*Quickly doffing*]
No, they are not all gone, Simon.

SAVOISY
You speak?

RICHARD/SIMON
We pray God will you preserve...

SAVOISY
Very well.

RICHARD:
...from going to the devil.

SIMON
... by land.

[*Exit RICHARD*]

[*Exit SIMON*]

[*Enter Savoisy's page OLIVIER to tell him:*]

OLIVIER
The gate is closed, monseigneur.

SAVOISY
No, Olivier. It is nine o'clock.

OLIVIER
No, monseigneur, it is tight shut.

[*Enter RAOUL with his PAGE who goes before*]

SAVOISY
What is this, Raoul?

RAOUL
What?

SAVOISY
The Louvre closed?

RAOUL
Wait. They will open.

SAVOISY
It is a fine morning. Walk with me.

RAOUL
Arbeletrier!

ARBALÉTRIER
Monseigneur?

RAOUL
Know why the gate is not open?

ARBALÉTRIER
Non, monseigneur.

SAVOISY/RAOUL
Non?

[*Enter DE PIERREFONDS*]

DE PIERREFONDS
Salut, messires.

It appears the queen holds court
from her balcony this morning.

SAVOISY
Ah! You divine it so...
[*Crossing himself*]
...seigneur de Pierrefonds! *Oui!*

[*Enter BURIDAN, impressive, with five MEN-at-ARMS*]

BURIDAN
Stay here!

SAVOISY
Excite your divine gift more. Who
is this fresh come with a half
lance of men; a *conducteur*, a *chef
d'escadre*, judge and executioner to
rival de Marigny, marquis, duke?

DE PIERREFONDS
I know him not.
Perhaps some Italian *condottiere*,
seeks his fortune.

SAVOISY
Seek? This *fanfaron* will seize.

[*BURIDAN contemplates them, nods*]

BURIDAN
And will hold what he seizes.
[*Another nod*]
Messeigneurs.

[*SAVOISY, DE PIERREFONDS, RAOUL huddle*]

DE PIERREFONDS
I hear that Belial voice!

RAOUL/SAVOISY
Moi aussi!

[*SAVOISY sees off:*]

SAVOISY
Seigneur de Marigny comes, to mount
Christian guard with us!

[*Enter DE MARIGNY*]

DE MARIGNY
Why do you not enter the palace?

BURIDAN
I will tell you, monseigneur.
An arrest is to be made. The palace
is closed to asylum.

DE MARIGNY
Arrest? I know not of an arrest!

BURIDAN
Here, monseigneur.
[*The parchment and seal*]
For your improvement: read.

SAVOISY
Farewell compliment, things
complicate...

DE MARIGNY
Give it me.

BURIDAN
Read it loud.

DE MARIGNY
"By this order of Marguerite, Queen
reigning and regent of France, that
Buridan, captain of Burgundy shall
arrest, seize hold Enguerrand de
Marigny, where found."

BURIDAN
C'est moi. Buridan, captain of
Burgundy.

DE MARIGNY
By the Queen's ordering?

BURIDAN
Your sword!

DE MARIGNY
Take it from its scabbard. It is
without stain.
[*The sword*]
When the hangman kicks me, soul
from body, it will fly up pure as
my sword.

BURIDAN
To the Chateau Vincennes!

DE MARIGNY
From there?

BURIDAN
Montfaucon will serve.
Where you took care erect a gibbet,
their inspiration there, it is but
just you try it.

DE MARIGNY
Captain, it was erect for criminals
not martyrs.

[*Crosses himself*] Thy will be done.

SAVOISY
Eh bien! Next it will be sorcery
captivates him.

DE PIERREFONDS
Abracadabra! The gates open!
[*Enter GAULTIER with five ARBALÉTRIER*]

SAVOISY
To let out, not in.

GAULTIER
Are you Buridan?
[*BURIDAN greets GAULTIER with a friendly nod*]

BURIDAN
You know me Gaultier. I am before
you, safe and well.

GAULTIER
You, who stood with my brother...

BURIDAN
I did. It is ten o'clock, have you
the book I gave you?

GAULTIER
... are suspect and accused of his
murder.

BURIDAN
Ah!
[*Laughs*] It is me she will have?

GAULTIER
It was you took him to his death.
[*The warrant*] Read. Read it loud.

BURIDAN

"By this order of Marguerite, Queen
reigning and regent of France, that
Gaultier d'Aulnay shall arrest..."

Are you not come to me on your oath
Gaultier, give to a priest of Saint
Francis? It is ten o'clock.

GAULTIER

Your sword!

BURIDAN

My order book!

GAULTIER

Your book?

BURIDAN

Oui, do you not have it?
[*Given the book*]

I would have taken it from you as
we agreed but now there is that
which must...
[*Holding it - elated*]
...be said before you arrest me.

[*BURIDAN opening the book*]

SAVOISY

We arrest the world today!

[*BURIDAN with the note book open, his elation turning to
consternation*]

BURIDAN

Gaultier! From this book a page is
torn...

GAULTIER

Then it is so.

BURIDAN

Who?

GAULTIER

Who?

[*He looks up at the balcony in confusion. MARGUERITE is not there*]

BURIDAN

My blood is on your head.

GAULTIER

Me?

BURIDAN

Look. See, a page ripped out!

What was writ, Gaultier?

GAULTIER

I know not.
[*Again up at the balcony*]

BURIDAN

Marguerite! You gave it the queen.

GAULTIER

I admit I did.

BURIDAN

So. *Eh bien.*

[*Enter MARGUERITE on balcony*]

GAULTIER

What was written?

BURIDAN

It is gone.

GAULTIER

What?

MARGUERITE

Remove that man to the prison,
grand Chatelet!

GAULTIER

What was written?

BURIDAN

Gone. Written in your brother's
blood, signed by your brother,
written by your brother...

MARGUERITE

Take him off!

GAULTIER

What? Tell me...

BURIDAN

It said: "Gaultier d'Aulnay is a
man without faith, without honour.
He cannot keep for one day that
which is give him in trust to his
honour and his faith!"
[*GAULTIER in scorn*]
There you have it, what it said,
faithless gentleman.
[*To MARGUERITE*]
Salut! Marguerite!

[*With DE MARIGNY's sword BURIDAN salutes MARGUE-
RITE. GAULTIER wary, steps back drawing his own
sword. BURIDAN turns to the young man and goes on
guard. GAULTIER thrusts at BURIDAN who parries with
the prime Parade and disarms him neatly by taking the
young man's sword under his left arm in a Disarm on the
Carte. This done, looking at the ARBALÉTRIER who have
raised their crossbows, BURIDAN tosses both swords at
GAULTIER to catch and presents his own sword, first
offering it to MARGUERITE:*]

BURIDAN

Marguerite! To you the first pass,
a parry and a disarm, but to me the
counter thrust *en revanche*, I hope.
[*To the ARBALÉTRIER*]
Messiers.

[*Exit BURIDAN with GAULTIER and escort*]

[*Exit MARGUERITE from the balcony*]

[*CHAMBERLAINS, GUARDS, ATTENDANTS open the gates, the windows, the doors of the palace. They call:* "Faites ouvrir les appartements! La Reine! La Reine!" *SAVOISY shakes his head in confusion*]

SAVOISY
Messeigneurs. We had best attend
the Queen!

[*Exeunt OMNES. Music*]

Curtain

ACT TWO

*Music. The sound of twelve
iron bound doors clanging
shut, chains, groans*

The curtain rises

SCENE 1

*A dungeon in the prison
grand Chatelet
Night*

[*Darkness. When light comes a chimney of slime encrusted
stone is seen going up and up, stone steps spiralling. Far
above there is a tiny grating through which ordure drips
and sometimes flows. BURIDAN discovered, alone, bound,
lying on the ground - he twists and thrashes and arches up
in his bonds - under the chimney. He whispers hoarsely:*]

                    BURIDAN
A man took hold tight my hand,
whispered "*courage*".
[*He calls*]
Are you there? Who were you?
[*Echoes*]
I know him not, could not see him.
[*Calls*]
Who are you?
[*Echo*]
It is enough, the heart leaps, a
friend! There is a friend will
bring fresh water, fresh bread, a
priest at my death, for death it

will be, soon, she cannot let me
live, will not...
[*Calls*] Who are you?

[*Echo*]
Down the steps, one hundred and
twenty, twelve doors slammed...
[*Calls*]
Allons!
[*Echo - he shouts in anger, twisting*]
...*allons!* Buridan! *Allons!*
[*Angrily*]
You have an account with Satan long
and intricate, set it right in your
mind, your conscience... insane!
[*Calls*]
Insanity!
[*Echo*]
I know the honour of men.

Men shriek honour and turn and run,
men sob honour while it pumps from
them with their blood.

Man's honour, like glass, shatters
at the compliant laugh; like snow,
it melts in the heat of a woman.
[*Calls*]
Insane! I have suspended my life
on such a gossamer thread as man's
honour... insane insane insane
insane insane insane insane, a
hundred times, a thousand times,
insaaaaaaaaaaaaaaane!
[*Echo echo echo*]
How she mocks, in the arms of that
faithless perfidious abject knave
Gaultier.... Gaultieeeeeeer! Each

kiss snatched from him should tear
her heart, his heart reproach,
remorse, compunction, sorrow!

Whilst I... me... me, I roll and
rail and struggle, bound, on cold
stone, earth, under the soil, in
this tomb...
[*Roars*]
Insane! I should have stretched
him, laid him, struck him down and
removed him from out this world.
[*Laugh*]
It is possible!
[*A glim of light up high*]
I see a single star in a dark sky,
just one to guide me, despairing
traveller that I am. She. She.

She will want to see and, insult my
death with her presence - that is
the star I see.

You demons who sculpt the hearts of
women with mallet and chisel, I beg
you have not left ungraved that
perversity of sentiment I augurate
will have her come... the queen.
[*Anguish - the light out*]
Oh it is a little star and it is
gone *out!*
[*Fury*]
Out! Out! Out!

Who were you?

[*The echoes, creak of a door opening*]

[*Chink of light again now near and on the level of
BURIDAN. The huge bulk of LANDRY fills the doorway*]

[*Enter LANDRY. He whispers, dimming the light:*]

LANDRY

Capitaine, ou êtes vous?

BURIDAN

Ici. Qui va la!

LANDRY

C'est moi. Ami.

BURIDAN

Qui, toi? I cannot see.

LANDRY

A friend need not be seen to be
known!

BURIDAN

Landry, again you come I am saved!

LANDRY

Impossible!

BURIDAN

What do you here then?

LANDRY

I am a gaoler.

BURIDAN

Gaoler here, assassin at the Tour
de Nesle... what employment!

LANDRY

Oui, enough.

BURIDAN

Durst thou do nothing? Shall you not
get me my priest?

LANDRY

No, but I can hear your confession,
and give it word for word to your
priest; and, what penance he gives,
word as a soldier... it, I shall
as well do for you, every word.

BURIDAN
Imbecile! Something to write upon?

LANDRY
Impossible!

BURIDAN
My purse.

LANDRY
Oui.

BURIDAN
Here, this pocket...
[*A purse*]
Spill it out. Count it. How much is
given you as gaoler?

LANDRY
Six livres a year. *Parisis!*

BURIDAN
Count the gold while I consider.
[*LANDRY counts*]
Have you counted it?

LANDRY
Have you considered?

BURIDAN
Oui, how much?

LANDRY
Three gold marcs.

BURIDAN
One hundred and sixty five livres.

LANDRY
Parisis?

BURIDAN
Tournois. But that is twenty eight
years labour in this prison.

Swear to me on your hope for heaven
you will do what I prescribe and
this sum is for you. It is all. Had
I more, it would be more.

LANDRY

Et vous?

BURIDAN

If they hang me, which is likely,
the hangman will pay for my cold
interring and I shall not need it
but, if I save myself you will have
four times as much... and, me, a
thousand times.

LANDRY

What?

BURIDAN

Go to my lodgings, my room, shut
yourself secret within, count the
stones from the corner where you
see a crucifix stand.

[*LANDRY crosses himself*]

On the seventh stone, a cross.

[*Crosses himself again*]

Your dagger, prise it up. In sand,
you will find a small iron box, the
key to it in this purse, open
it... you may assure yourself it
contains only papers, not gold.

If tomorrow when the King comes to
Paris you see me not safe, sound,
and saying to you "Give me the box
and the key", you will, down on
your knees give both, to Louis and,
if I am dead I am thus revenged.

That is all; my soul will rest, it
will be to you I owe thanks and the
bitch will smother!

LANDRY

You may place your trust in me.

BURIDAN

On your eternal soul?

LANDRY

On it as I hope for paradise, I do
swear.

BURIDAN

Adieu, Landry. Try to be an honest
man.

LANDRY

I shall try, *capitaine*.
[*Going then coming back*]
Mais... mais c'est bien difficile.

[*Exit LANDRY. The light is taken up by LANDRY, and the
twelve doors slam*]

BURIDAN

Allons! allons! Come hangman,
come noose, vengeance is crouched
at the foot of the tree.

Vengeance! A word, merry, sublime
from living lips, deep sonorous and
empty from the grave and which, no
matter how loud it re-echoes...

[*Calls*] Echo-echo-echo!
[*Echo echo echo*]
...can never wake the corpse laid
in a tomb....

[*Calls*] I am tombed!
[*Echo*]

[A small and secret door opens silently from another cell.
Enter MARGUERITE. ORSINI waits in the cell]

ORSINI

Attento...!

MARGUERITE

Is he bound?

ORSINI

Tight. Limb to limb and chain to
stone.

[BURIDAN sees the light]

BURIDAN

Qui va la?

MARGUERITE

Orsini, wait. Should I cry - come
with lance straight for his heart.

[Hand out] The knife!

BURIDAN

Qui va la?

[ORSINI gives her a knife, goes back into the cell to watch
and wait]

MARGUERITE

C'est moi!

[BURIDAN utters a deep sigh "Aaaaaaaaaaaaaagh"]

BURIDAN

You are come.

Lantern lit you seek shivering
pleasure still, my death, in
glorious, voluptuous certainty of
your triumph.

Oh wanton woman, oh epicurean
woman, *a moi! a moi!* here to me!

MARGUERITE

No prayer you utter will melt my
heart...

BURIDAN
I utter none, none...

MARGUERITE
...in vain...

BURIDAN
...but I excite you more.

MARGUERITE
...love, Buridan, lodged deep in a
young man's heart will gnaw corrode
those other puerilities honour,
faith, oaths of loyalty - sworn to.

Love diseases. You foolish put your
trust in a man sick of it from his
scalp to his scrotum.
[*A lantern*]
You would have him read this piece
of paper"I die assassinate by the
hand of Marguerite..."
[*The paper*]
See! See! Look! Death...
[*She burns it*]
...last flames, last hope! Am I
free now, Buridan?

You are arrest for the murder of
Philippe d'Aulnay... not I.

BURIDAN
But I know a secret.

MARGUERITE
There are poisons of such terrible
violence they shatter their phials,
such are your secrets, take care of
your heart... which contains them.

Who will you tell?

BURIDAN

Marguerite, come closer your body.
I will tell.

MARGUERITE

Too late, I am gone.

BURIDAN

I shall wail your name at my
trial...

MARGUERITE

Trial? No trial for a man like you
...a priest...

BURIDAN

...moan your name at my hanging.

MARGUERITE

Hanging? No hangman for you... a
priest... and a bully for you,
the priest starts it, the bully
ends it here, this dirty place,
here your last place on earth,
where the walls deaden anguish, put
out sobs, choke cries, here is
where you will convulse your
last... strangled by your own hand
- ever known to be incontrovertible
proof of guilt.

BURIDAN

Then shall I whisper my secret to
myself... if you come close you
might hear it, if you go you will
not and... you will wonder.

[*MARGUERITE going*]

[*BURIDAN whispers and she stops, not sure what she has
heard. ORSINI comes out. She turns her back, closes the
door on ORSINI. She stands by the door and the whispers
of BURIDAN stay whispers but become louder, and louder
and more seductive, she curves her body towards him and
hears:*]

> BURIDAN
>
> ...Duke Robert, of Burgundy... a
> beautiful young daughter - her body
> that of an angel, her soul that of
> a demon... her name...

[*The whispers fade*]

[*MARGUERITE whispers also:*]

> MARGUERITE
>
> Her name...?

> BURIDAN
>
> ...a page with a heart frank and
> open and trusting...

> MARGUERITE
>
> Her name...?

> BURIDAN
>
> ...whose name was Lyonnet de
> Bournonville... and they loved.
>
> It is a strange story, they loved
> but none knew, each night he came
> and each morning he went...
>
> [*He groans*]
>
> I am... I am... help me to change
> round to the other side to lie. I
> am in such pain this side...
>
> [*She does*]
>
> ...merci, merci...
>
> [*He smiles his thanks*]
>
> She told him in tears, Lyonnet de
> Bournonville, that she was with
> child, in her womb, Marguerite.
>
> And her father the Duke sped her to
> a convent, Marguerite.
>
> But first a last tryst of tears,
> before the doors of the convent

closed for ever, as if her tomb,
Marguerite.

For her, to be her tomb.

Oh, this was a hideous night, they
clung and they cried and looked at
a... dagger and they...

Please! Please... these ropes...

MARGUERITE
What did they do?

BURIDAN
...bite my flesh and pain, such
pain.

A dagger.

She held it like you hold that
knife, and she said"Lyonnet, Lyonnet,
if this time tomorrow my
father ... "
[*Groans*]
Pity, I beg you, cut these ropes.

[*On impulse MARGUERITE cuts the rope which binds his
arms and BURIDAN gives a sigh and a laugh and says no
more*]

MARGUERITE
What more?

[*BURIDAN looks at her, says nothing. She bends over him
and laughing softly, BURIDAN continues:*]

BURIDAN
"...if tomorrow my father is
dead, there need be no convent,
no parting, only love, our love..."

The dagger passed from her hands to
the hands of the page. In the dark
his arm taken and, like led through
the paths of hell... a hand lifts

a curtain... the page armed, the
duke asleep.

The noble head of the old man, calm
asleep and serene, seen so for ever
by his assassin page, in his dreams
and in his waking hours for ever,
in infamy... for ever...

Marguerite, the young and beautiful
Marguerite, entered not a convent,
not she... Queen of Navarre, Queen
of France - she!

MARGUERITE
Me.

BURIDAN
You.

Next day, by hand of one Orsini,
the page had a letter sent him, and
gold. Marguerite bid him hence for
ever - after their vile crime they
must never meet again.

MARGUERITE
A letter, how imprudent.

BURIDAN

A girl she was then, would not now.

Some last compunction, some guilt
of conscience had her set it down
in all its shocking complicity and,
in her hand and, her name.

MARGUERITE
He went, did he not, Lyonnet de
Bournonville, never to be seen
again, he and the letter lost?
How may this concern a queen?

BURIDAN
You know how it may.

The letter will be the first
petition of Louis the Tenth of
France, his entry into Paris,
tomorrow.

You gloat me what the punishment is
for murderers Marguerite, now hear
how a parricide and an adulteress
will die.

Hair is shaved with red hot shears.
They are opened, living, for to
draw the heart out, which is burnt,
cinders flung to the wind.

Three days after, the mutilate body
is took through Paris on a hurdle.

MARGUERITE
Grâce! grâce!

BURIDAN
These ropes, my hands, another
service you may do... my hands.
[*She cuts ropes*]
Fetch in priest and bully, here is
the garrot!
[*The rope*]

And tomorrow the cry "Buridan,
murderer of Philippe d'Aulnay
strangled in prison...!"

Another cry heard answer from the
Louvre:"Marguerite de Bourgogne is
to die for adultery and parricide."

MARGUERITE
Have pity Buridan...

BURIDAN
I am Buridan no more!

[*Cries*]

I am Lyonnet de Bournonville,
Marguerite's page, the killer of
Robert of Burgundy - his master,
and her noble father!

MARGUERITE

You cry out! You will be heard.

BURIDAN

What do you fear? These slimed
walls deaden anguish, put out sobs,
choke cries...

MARGUERITE

What is to be done?

BURIDAN

Again?

MARGUERITE

Oui... what?

BURIDAN

You ride tomorrow on the right of
the King, I shall ride on his left.

MARGUERITE

So be it. I shudder but say it.

BURIDAN

C'est bien.

MARGUERITE

The letter?

BURIDAN

When the letter is offered the king
I take it, as his first minister.

MARGUERITE

De Marigny is not yet dead.

BURIDAN

You swore...

MARGUERITE
He has an hour to live.

BURIDAN
Eh bien.
[Stopping her going]
Wait. The child?

MARGUERITE
Child? Chi... I gave to a man.

BURIDAN
His name?

MARGUERITE
I forget.

BURIDAN
Think Marguerite, and you will
remember.

MARGUERITE
Landry, I think. Orsini? A man.

BURIDAN
Landry! Landry!

MARGUERITE
What do you do?

BURIDAN
Orsini!

MARGUERITE
He is not...

[Enter ORSINI]

BURIDAN
Orsini.

MARGUERITE
... here.

BURIDAN
Approach Orsini. I am first
minister of France.

Assure him, Marguerite.

MARGUERITE
It is true, he is first minister.

ORSINI
Command me, *maresciallo*.

BURIDAN
The lamp, a star to light us...
[*To MARGUERITE*]
Take my arm, madame.

MARGUERITE
Where do we go?

BURIDAN
To meet before our King, Louis the
Tenth in triumphal entry to Paris.

Alla luce delle stelle...!

[*Exeunt OMNES, the doors open to keys and clang, all twelve of them*]

[*Music*]

SCENE 2

The banks of the River Seine
Day

[*Double tower of the Tour de Nesle, a hidden quay and steps up from the river. City wall. Gate of Saint-Honore. Boats*]

[*Heard off: Fanfare. Drums, trumpets, bagpipes and cymbals. A clamour of horse, foot, shout: "Noel! Noel!" that is the triumphal entry of KING LOUIS X into Paris. Horses, lances, banners shadows across the scene. Crescendo of noise and then fading*]

SCENE 3

Private apartments of the
Queen in the Louvre
Day

[*MARGUERITE appears to be asleep on her bed. Music. Sound of birds, shafts of sunlight through curtains. She lies in sumptuousness*]

[*Enter GAULTIER through a secret door. He approaches the bed, on tip-toe, sits at the head, speaks very softly, gently and sadly:*]

GAULTIER

Oh my queen, how I longed the night
 through my duty, for sun to rise,
to break, to warm the morning so
that I might wake you softly, with
my love, this last time... my
brother gone now none but you, what
consolation I have is you...

CHARLOTTE

Seigneur!

[*CHARLOTTE sits up on the bed. GAULTIER bewildered*]

GAULTIER

Where sleeps the queen?

CHARLOTTE

Has she not returned?
[*Off the bed*]
That she has not or I would not be
here, in her bed...

She took her cloak I gave her, last
night, but where I know not...

She left me wait and, wearying of
her return, I lay upon her bed and

slept, until I heard such sweet
words, so softly spoke... I woke.

I thought I was... you woke me...
seigneur... in heaven.

[*GAULTIER is distraught*]

GAULTIER

Not returned? How could she not
return? Where could she go that
she went the night... where has
she slept, where does she wake?

[*CHARLOTTE screams as GAULTIER draws his sword*]

CHARLOTTE

Seigneur, I am not to blame, no,
please, your anger play elsewhere.

I know not where she went.

[*GAULTIER puts his sword up. Ashamed at his action*]

GAULTIER

Forgive me, Charlotte, she would
once tell you, as once me, every
thing.
[*Dejection*]
This is a dagger to my heart.
[*Angry he accuses*]
She gave you secret where!

CHARLOTTE

Would she had, your anger has me
fear for her. What I knew I would
tell - but nothing do I know.

We are hers, and used we to know
all, but there is one knows more,
has known her since a child...

He, the Italian, Orsini, has often
secret consortation with her and is
admit when he demands, her command.

GAULTIER

Yes, he!

[*Going*]

Open the apartments Charlotte and,
forgive me my brutality.

[*Exit GAULTIER*]

CHARLOTTE

Bon courage, monseigneur! I pray
for you.

[*Opens the curtains, the doors, the bed*]

[*The cry goes up*:"Faites ouvrir les appartements! Faites
ouvrir les appartements!"]

[*Doors opened in the palace, one room to another by
GUARDS and a few COURTIERS enter*]

SCENE 4

Chamber in the Louvre, balcony
Day

[*Enter DE PIERREFONDS and SAVOISY*]

SAVOISY

You wait not on Louis,
his triumphal entry, de Pierrefonds?

DE PIERREFONDS

No, I wait upon Marguerite, her way
shall be mine.

SAVOISY

I wait him here as well...

For there is such a great flowing
of loyal people I fear drowning -

it being in fashion - in the muddy
ooze of loyal love.

If the queen go, I too, with you.

DE PIERREFONDS
It is just possible Savoisy, you
think the king to be the queen, not
the king she greets...

SAVOISY
It is.

DE PIERREFONDS
It is?

SAVOISY
Just. It would be.

[*Enter RAOUL*]

DE PIERREFONDS
Bonjour, baron. What of the king?

RAOUL
He comes, marshals, flags, banners
and pursuivant at arms before, the
queen rides at his side...

[*Cries heard outside:* "Vive le roi! Vive le roi!"]

RAOUL
[*Continued*]... on his right.

DE PIERREFONDS
Then we are not right placed.

SAVOISY
We left it too late.

RAOUL
At his left hand...

SAVOISY
I would be glad told, not Gaultier
d'Aulnay...!

RAOUL

Then rejoice! Not anywhere.

SAVOISY

What? Not?

Bid them drag the river messieurs
down from the Tower of Nesle, for
he is as pretty as his brother.

RAOUL

He who rides in place of Gaultier
is the Italian *condottiere*, he,
arrest by Gaultier and thrown in
the prison of grand Chatelet.

Unpunished - to my sight, not a
mark, complete with eyes, with
nose, with ears, with lights, with a
head stuck firm on shoulders out
his sweetly worn armour - not even
flogged, he.

DE PIERREFONDS

What say you to that, Savoisy?

SAVOISY

We live in very strange times. On
yesterday de Marigny was first
minister, today not, but arrested.

Likewise yesterday, the captain
arrested, today he rides where de
Marigny would ride, in complete
possession of his limbs and neck.

RAOUL

And lights.

DE PIERREFONDS

Sorcery. I declare it!

God jousts with Satan for the
kingdom of France!

[*Cries from outside, nearer:* "Noel! Noel! vive le roi!"]

[*Enter GUARDS, MARSHALS, a POURSUIVANT at ARMS
with the arms of France emblazoned to warn:*]

POURSUIVANT
Le roi, messieurs, le roi!

[*Enter LOUIS X. Music*]

LOUIS X
Salut, messeigneurs, salut!

We are blessed with fine soldiers
fight for us in Champagne and, as I
count, many fine courtiers here.

SAVOISY
Sire, the day soldiers and court
march together against our enemies
will be a great day for France.

LOUIS X
That we might the better march
together on campaign I give order
that a tax be levied on the city of
Paris, as celebrate my entry.

[*To the balcony, a wave:* "Vive le roi! Vive le roi!"]

Oui, mes enfants, I shall cut all
taxes in measure of my love for
you, *mes enfants...* subjects... my
people!

[*Enter BURIDAN and MARGUERITE*]

BURIDAN
Remember. To we two the power, we
two are France!

[From without" *Vive le roi! Vive le roi!*"]

LOUIS X
Oui oui, mes enfants.
[*To BURIDAN*]
De Bournonville, you will raise a
new tax from the trades and guilds

of Paris in order that this tax
will pay for the old tax I have at
a stroke abolished - one will pay
for the other and it will be just.

[*Leaving the window he says to all the Court:*]

Messeigneurs, here is my hand waits
its bathe in your kisses!

[*LOUIS X puts out his hand. SAVOISY, DE PIERRE-FONDS, RAOUL and other COURTIERS rush to kiss the hand of the king*]

[*Music*]

[*PETITIONERS are admitted. They enter and cry:* "Vive le roi! Vive le roi!" *GUARDS hold them back in an entrance. Among them LANDRY, transfixed with awe at sight of the king. BURIDAN extricates LANDRY from the other PETITIONERS and takes him aside. LANDRY's gaze never leaves the king*]

BURIDAN

I am here. You see.

I say to you, "Give me the box, and
the key!"

[*LANDRY disappointed...*]

LANDRY

You are safe?

BURIDAN

Oui.

[*...but lives in hope*]

LANDRY

You are not harmed?

BURIDAN

I am not harmed. Safe, sound and I
say to you, "Give me box and key!"
[*A thought*]
You have it?

LANDRY
You have the twelve marcs?

BURIDAN
Tonight.

LANDRY
Where?

BURIDAN
At my lodgings.

LANDRY
Tonight I will give it you. I will
give you the box and the key if you
are safe and...

BURIDAN
There are many things I have need
question you, many...

LANDRY
I will answer all.

BURIDAN
C'est bien.

LANDRY
I would have liked to go down on my
knees before the king.

[*Exit LANDRY reluctantly*]

[*Enter GAULTIER, rashly approaches the queen, whispers:*]

GAULTIER
Madame, where slept you?

MARGUERITE
Gaultier!

GAULTIER
Tell me.

MARGUERITE
Gaultier, take care!

[*GAULTIER sees BURIDAN, exclaims:*]

GAULTIER

Buridan, here?

What does he, here?

[*GAULTIER, hand on sword, prevented from reaching BURIDAN by the queen who whispers to him urgently, a hand on his arm:*]

MARGUERITE

Gaultier, I love you, you alone, I
shall love you for ever!

[*He breaks free of her, pushes through the COURTIERS who scatter, to reach BURIDAN, his sword half out of its scabbard. MARGUERITE says loudly, so all can hear:*]

MARGUERITE

Come, captain, and kiss the hand of
the king.
[*Again*] Come!

[*GAULTIER confused. The king, all the court looking at GAULTIER, waiting. BURIDAN lets his sword slide back. GAULTIER bows to MARGUERITE. He approaches and kisses the hand of LOUIS , who then smiles grimly at them all and says:*]

LOUIS X

Now it is time for me to rule,
messeigneurs, come those of you are
my council, come my queen, come
Lyonnet de Bournonville, the
kingdom awaits our consociation.

[*GUARDS push back the PETITIONERS who cry:* "Vive le roi! Vive le roi!" *POURSUIVANT at ARMS commands:*]

POURSUIVANT

Place au roi!

[*A sweep of COURTIERS, GUARDS, and exit LOUIS*]

POURSUIVANT

Place à la reine!

[*A sweep of COURTIERS and GUARDS and exit MARGUERITE*]

POURSUIVANT
Place au premier ministre!

[*Exit BURIDAN*]

[*Exit POURSUIVANT*]

SAVOISY
Lyonnet de Bournonville. That is not the name of a *condottiere!*

The name is old. It has fame.

I am awake, messeigneurs, do you assure me?

If I am not I shall be be wakened, if I am I shall be sent off - what ever state, I am eager to see the finish of this thing.

Gaultier! You must know.

GAULTIER
Ask me not, messeigneurs, for I know nothing... ask me not!

[*Enter POURSUIVANT*]

POURSUIVANT
Le sire de Pierrefonds!

DE PIERREFONDS
Voici.

POURSUIVANT
Ordre du roi.

[*He hands DE PIERREFONDS a parchment with seal*]

[*Exit POURSUIVANT*]

[*DE PIERREFONDS reads, puzzled*]

DE PIERREFONDS
It is an order I shall repair to Vincennes, take up de Marigny our

once first minister, deliver him to
Mounfacon where, without doubt, he
will dangle from his own gibbet.
[*Regret*]
I never wished him well.

SAVOISY

Bien! The first order in council
of our king is a death warrant.

My compliments on your commission.

DE PIERREFONDS

I would have hoped for better than,
but, what I am commanded by my king
I shall accomplish.

Adieu, messieurs.

[*Exit a troubled DE PIERREFONDS*]

SAVOISY

Adieu...!

[*Enter POURSUIVANT with another parchment*]

POURSUIVANT

Le compte de Savoisy?

SAVOISY

Oh, oh, *voici.*

POURSUIVANT

Letters patentes du roi

[*Hands him the letters patent*]

[*Exit POURSUIVANT*]

RAOUL

What?

SAVOISY

Oui.

[*He holds the parchment*]

The first order makes me reluctant
to open the second for fear, who?
[*Waits*]
If it is an order of death for one
of us, you, it is better to delay.
[*A deep breath*]
But, this king brooks none.
[*Opens it*]
I am commissioned a captain of the
guard. Is there a place?

RAOUL

None but that give Gaultier.

[*SAVOISY looks at GAULTIER who stands alone at the balcony*]

SAVOISY

By God! I ever wished him well.

RAOUL

Nevertheless, you are congratulate.

SAVOISY

I am to safe guard the apartments.
That my task and appointment.
[*Reads*]
At once.
[*A relieved snigger*]
Then I durst not delay...
what it is to be favoured...
[*He laughs*]
So know the king is a great king,
the new first minister *nonpareil!*

[*Exit SAVOISY with an embarrassed glance at GAULTIER*]

[*Re-enter POURSUIVANT*]

POURSUIVANT
Sire Gaultier d'Aulnay!

GAULTIER

Hein?

POURSUIVANT

Lettres patentes du roi.

GAULTIER

Not she, but from the king?

[*GAULTIER given the letters patent. POURSUIVANT addresses the rest of the COURT*]

POURSUIVANT

Messeigneurs, the king, our lord
will not receive after the council,
you have his permit you may retire.

[*GAULTIER reading the letters patent*]

GAULTIER

"... command of the province of
Champagne... leave Paris at once
for Troyes!"

Me? Leave Paris? Command in
Champagne... why?

RAOUL

It is a step Gaultier, you are to
be congratulate, it is fair reward
and the queen could not equal it.

GAULTIER

Congratulate!

Then congratulate Satan, archangel
that he was, he now commands Hell!

I shall not go.

Were you not bid go? Then go. I
shall not...

[*Anger*] *Go!* The king did bid you go!

RAOUL

God protect you, Gaultier.

[*Exit RAOUL and all the COURTIERS hurriedly, leaving an angry GAULTIER, hand on sword, pacing, bewildered*]

GAULTIER

Go... I shall not go, bid leave
Paris! Me? Is this what I was
promised? I was not!

The ground moves, this is not
ground I have trod these last days,
for all about me things move, that
which I have held real, even as I
touch, vanishes... phantoms!

[*Enter MARGUERITE*]

MARGUERITE

Gaultier!

GAULTIER

It is you at last, madame!

Do you mock me that you promise and
then break your word?

Am I a child's toy - am I a child
for you to laugh at? But
yesterday you swore we would never
part, today I am hasten from Paris
to a province...!

MARGUERITE

It is not so.

GAULTIER

Not so? I have it here... how
could you?

MARGUERITE

I was forced, Gaultier.

GAULTIER

Forced! Who may force a queen?

MARGUERITE

A demon, with power.

GAULTIER
Who? Tell me...

MARGUERITE
You must seem to obey, at once,
go! Tomorrow, here, I will relate
the reasons for your banishment.

GAULTIER
You cannot expect I shall go on
such...

MARGUERITE
I can! I do.

GAULTIER
I will come back that you might
tell me better re-assurance.

MARGUERITE
Oui. Return tomorrow, Gaultier.
[*Looks off*]
Someone comes. Go, Gaultier!

GAULTIER
Remember this promise. *Adieu!*

[*Enter BURIDAN*]

BURIDAN
Forgive me my impediment to your
adieux, Marguerite.

MARGUERITE
You are mistaken, Buridan.

BURIDAN
Was that not Gaultier left you?

MARGUERITE
We said not *adieu*.

BURIDAN
Did you not?

MARGUERITE
He is not to leave.

BURIDAN
The king orders him gone.

MARGUERITE
I order him stay.

BURIDAN
You forget our covenant.

MARGUERITE
I promised you would be first
minister, you are, you promised me
Gaultier, now you send him go!

BURIDAN
We said we two would be France, you
now say we *three*, him also.

He cannot be brought party to our
confiding.

MARGUERITE
Notwithstanding, it will be.

BURIDAN
Have you forgotten I have you still
in my power?

MARGUERITE
Oui. But then it was when you were
Buridan, my prisoner.

You now are Lyonnet de Bournonville
...of France, first minister.

Destroy me, destroy yourself.

With your life give back to you,
you have honours, rank, riches and
power and... greater height from
which to fall!

We are together on a slippery crag,
you toss me from it and you must
follow, our cries heard mingle in
our plunged destruction.

BURIDAN

You love him?

MARGUERITE

More than life.

BURIDAN

I would have thought I could stamp
on your heart, crush it, hack it,
twist it, without risk of a single
drop of human feeling.

Love? You have been brought low,
Marguerite, that you search for it.

We are rulers of France, not any
more creatures of whim and fancy,
tears have no place in our eyes,
regret no place in our hearts and
love none, not it, not affection of
any kind lest we are surrendered.
I believed you to be a demon. I now
fear you to be only a fallen angel.

MARGUERITE

I shall not let him leave my side.

BURIDAN

Not...?
[*Aside*]
I am lost do I not destroy them
both
[*Aloud*]
Marguerite, if I tell you that your
love for this young man is for me
intolerable, in that it awakes me

memories of what was once our own
and; what you have seen in me as
ambition, the quest for vengeance
is... love, my love... oh if...?

And... if I tell you also, that
all that which I have gained is
only for one purpose; that we might
be as we were, the page Lyonnet and
the young Marguerite together again
as one, the letter give you back in
proof that what I now have is
naught but my desire to be once
again as we were.

If, if say, say, if, you find in me
this devotion, this love... say you
not now he must be sent, gone?

MARGUERITE
Is it true, or mockery, Lyonnet?

BURIDAN
Receive me tonight and tonight I
return you the letter but, not as
it has been, not hate, not menace,
no no, love, that love again.

Let us meet in love and tomorrow
you will have the letter and I not.

All I gain is rendered you back.

MARGUERITE
Should I...

If, if I do receive you, it cannot
be here at the palace.

BURIDAN
Can you not leave as you wish?

MARGUERITE
Where? Where might we...

BURIDAN
The Tower of Nesle?

MARGUERITE
...meet?
[*Taken aback*]
You would meet me there?

BURIDAN
Have I not already there met you
for just such purpose, our meeting
separate only by the caprice of a
veiled woman?

MARGUERITE
[*Aside*] He yields!

[*Aloud*] I confess to a weakening, a strange
frailty, Lyonnet... that happiness
there was... your voice evokes
souvenirs d'amor I had thought
dead, buried... deep in my heart.

BURIDAN
Marguerite!

MARGUERITE
Lyonnet!

BURIDAN
Gaultier will go hence?

MARGUERITE
Sent tonight, do you wish it.
[*A key*]
Here is a key will give you in by
the postern of the Tour de Nesle
[*She gives it him*]
I must leave
[*Going - a last aside*]

Ah! Buridan, this time you will
not escape.

[*Exit MARGUERITE, leaving BURIDAN with the key*]

BURIDAN

The key to your tomb, Marguerite.

But, be assured you shall not rot
in it alone!

[*Exit BURIDAN*]

SCENE 5

A garden at the Louvre
Day

[*Hedges, trees, the sound of the river lapping*]

[*Enter SAVOISY. BURIDAN heard off: "Compte de Savoisy!" SAVOISY stops and waits*]

[*Enter BURIDAN*]

BURIDAN

Compte de Savoisy.

SAVOISY

Me voici, monseigneur.

BURIDAN

Give this to Gaultier d'Aulnay.

[*BURIDAN hands SAVOISY a note. Then holds up a warrant bearing the royal seal*]

SAVOISY

Monseigneur.

[*SAVOISY tucks away the note*]

BURIDAN

There is this for you.

[*The warrant*]
The king pains to learn of the
night killings of young men,
Savoisy, which afflict the city.
He views with suspicion the Tower
of Nesle and orders you go there,
with a lance of ten men, at nine
o'clock tonight. You will seize and
detain all there found whatever
in title or rank.
[*Giving him the warrant*]
You have your warrant here.

SAVOISY
I have seigneur, my first!

I shall not prove tardy.

BURIDAN
That is as well, Savoisy!

[*Exit SAVOISY with great self importance*]

BURIDAN
For it is the most important order
he will ever discharge.

[*Exit BURIDAN*]

[*Enter MARGUERITE from the palace, towards the river,
through the garden. She stops at a hedge, calls softly:*]

MARGUERITE
Orsini? Orsini!

[*ORSINI appears from the hedge*]

ORSINI
Eccomi qua, regina!

MARGUERITE
Tonight, at the Tower, have four
armed men with you.

ORSINI
Benissimo, your orders?

MARGUERITE
Later I shall give them.

ORSINI
Signora.

[*Exit ORSINI*]

[*Exit MARGUERITE*]

SCENE 6

The lodgings of Buridan
Night

[*Crucifix. The stones. One of them prised up. The small box with a candle placed on it*]

[*Discovered LANDRY sitting on the stones, with wine, a piece of chalk, his legs out around the hole. He calculates*]

LANDRY
Twelve marcs, in gold. That is...
[*Chalking*]
....six hundred eighteen livres,
tournois, not *parisis, tournois.*

If the Captain keeps his promise
and gives me the twelve marcs in
gold, six hundred eighteen livres,
for this box, *tournois,* for which I
would not give six sous *parisis,* I
shall heed his exhortation advice
and become an honest man - at once.

But, what, how, when I am without a
trade that is honest?

For soldier is not, for what he is
asked to do.
[*A sorrowful sigh*]

He must kill, rape and loot to the
best of his ability - at once.

[*Brightening*]

Ma foi! With six hundred eighteen
livres, *tournois*, I shall raise a
company, captain of it in service
of some grand seigneur.

I shall pocket all he gives me and
order my men they must get their
needs from dishonesty - at once.

That I might live honest.

Vive Dieu! That is honest. There
will be honest wine and... who is
it cares for an honest woman?

Under the cross we shall do good
works, assist those we meet with
too much gold or goods to enter the
kingdom of heaven - where they will
get their just reward - in poverty.

At once!

Sang-Dieu! If I am not mistaken a
happy and honest life and I need
not leave my trade! We shall ever
on my strict orders carry out the
duties of Christian soldiers in
regard to sorcerers, gypsies, Jews;
and flay their skin from them, easy
as swallow a glass of wine.

[*Enter BURIDAN*]

                    BURIDAN
C'est bien, Landry.

                    LANDRY
I am here.

                    BURIDAN
You drink?

LANDRY
No better companion.

BURIDAN
Gold buys wine.

LANDRY
Here is your box.

BURIDAN
Here is your twelve marcs.

LANDRY
Merci.

BURIDAN
Now, I have to meet a young man
here.

[*A crash heard off. LANDRY sniggers*]

LANDRY
The old stairs.

BURIDAN
Let him in.

[*LANDRY goes out the door. Heard off:* "Le capitaine
Buridan?" *BURIDAN calls:* "Le voici"]

[*Enter GAULTIER*]

GAULTIER
Well?

BURIDAN
I am no longer Buridan.

I am Lyonnet de Bournonville, first
minister of Louis the Tenth.

GAULTIER
It matters not what title you usurp.

BURIDAN
Usurp?

Why, are you not gone to Champagne?

GAULTIER
I am ordered not, by the queen.

BURIDAN
The queen?

GAULTIER
Oui.

[*BURIDAN holds the box, turns the key and opens it*]

BURIDAN
I sent for you for the oath you
took, Gaultier d'Aulnay to come to
me even from the knees of your
mistress - is it she you left?

GAULTIER
It is not.
I came to you not for that oath,
for that oath died with my brother.

BURIDAN
Yet I did him service.

GAULTIER
I came for what you promised.

BURIDAN
What was that? The name of your
brother's murderer, how de Marigny
went to his death... what?

GAULTIER
No no not that, none of that, God
will avenge my brother, God will
avenge de Marigny... her.

You promised me I might see her!

BURIDAN
So you care not for anything else?

GAULTIER
God forgive me. I want her.

BURIDAN

What use am I for that? Can you
not enter by a secret door in an
alcove... you shake. Is it rage
has you do it, or is it that this
night Marguerite, like another
night sleeps not in the Louvre?

GAULTIER

Who told you?

BURIDAN

The man with whom she passed the
night.

GAULTIER

Blasphemy! You are insane!

BURIDAN

Take care, young man, take your
hand from your sword.
[*His hand on his own*]
Marguerite is a beautiful and
passionate woman.

Writes she to you?

GAULTIER

What need you know of that?

BURIDAN

Are her words enchanting and ardent
and passionately persuasive, is her
hand round and clear and deep cut?

GAULTIER

That you shall not know, your eyes
will never light on the sacred...

[*BURIDAN holds out a letter from the box. GAULTIER
glances at it, at once recognises the hand of MARGUERITE.
He gasps*]

BURIDAN

Read: "Your beloved friend
Marguerite."

Oui?

GAULTIER

It is falsely done! It is
infernal.

BURIDAN

Is it not tempting - when near to
her, when she talks to you of love,
when you gently run your hand in
her long hair she lets flow undone
voluptuously about her - to cut a
tress, like this?

[*From the box, a tress of hair*]

[*GAULTIER confused*]

GAULTIER

It is the way she writes. It is her
hair. Stolen!

BURIDAN

Ask that of her.

GAULTIER

Where? At once!

BURIDAN

Not here, she is elsewhere.

GAULTIER

Where? This instant!

BURIDAN

She has a *rendezvous*.

GAULTIER

She has a *rendezvous* with whom?
[*Hand at sword hilt*]
I thirst for his blood, his life!

> BURIDAN

Take care.

[*Smiling - his sword*]

If he is finished his desire for
her - and will cede you rights?

> GAULTIER

Me?

> BURIDAN

Oui.

[*Shrugs and yawns*]

He tires of her, has compassion for
you and, will give you free of her.

[*GAULTIER draws his sword in rage. BURIDAN his*]

> GAULTIER

How dare you!

[*GAULTIER lunges at BURIDAN who parries, steps to the
side and waits for another lunge which he parries again,
and again. They fight silently, GAULTIER unable to find
a way through BURIDAN's guard, until BURIDAN disarms
him. BURIDAN with the tip of his sword at GAULTIER's
heart, drops on one knee - eyes on GAULTIER all the time
- picks up GAULTIER's sword, hands it back to him*]

> BURIDAN

Young man. Tonight you will need a
sword.

[*GAULTIER accepts the sword and BURIDAN steps back,
stays on guard*]

> GAULTIER

O mon Dieu!

[*GAULTIER sheathes his sword and BURIDAN lowers his
guard*]

> BURIDAN

It is past eight o'clock and
Marguerite waits... for, Gaultier?

GAULTIER
Where is she?

BURIDAN
The Tower of Nesle.

GAULTIER
[*Going*] *Bien...*

BURIDAN
You forget the key to postern and
inner door.

GAULTIER
Give it!

BURIDAN
One more word... or so.

GAULTIER
Speak.

BURIDAN
It is she who killed your brother.

[*GAULTIER looks at him aghast, hand flying to sword
again. BURIDAN smiles gently. GAULTIER collapses,
staggers from the room, crying:*]

GAULTIER
Oh wicked wicked...!

[*Exit GAULTIER leaving BURIDAN alone*]

BURIDAN
C'est bien!

Go meet again, find each the other,
brother through lover.
[*Calls*] Landry!
Landry... I know you skulk!

[*Enter LANDRY*]

LANDRY
Capitaine. At once!

BURIDAN
First, that young man, he goes to
the Tower of Nesle, how long?

LANDRY
Does he have a boat?

BURIDAN
No.

LANDRY
Half an hour.

BURIDAN
C'est bien, the glass.

[*LANDRY gives BURIDAN the hour glass. BURIDAN turns
it, settles so that he might watch it. Yawns*]

BURIDAN
I would talk of war in Italy.

LANDRY
Monseigneur? *Cric!*

BURIDAN
Crac! Drink, and talk.

LANDRY
Oui.

Bitter wars and good times. Days
passed in battle, nights in orgy.

As the cellar of the Prior of Genoa
we drank dry, to the last drop.

Such as the convent of young girls
we fucked dry to the last old nun.
[*He crosses himself*]
Days of great joy and great sins.

BURIDAN
The day we die, our sins on scales
against our good deeds, I hope you
can tap it that our good deeds tip.

LANDRY
I will need know them.
[*He hinks hard*]
I have some... of that I am sure.

BURIDAN
Search your past, sergeant. Humour
me of children...

LANDRY
Oui.

It was in Germany, a child, poor
little angel. Hope he prays for me.
[*A tear wiped*]
We pursued Bohemians, as you know,
pagans, idolaters and infidels.

On their filthy heels, some cuts we
got, a few, and then while a
village burned I heard the sweetest
sound, a poor little pagan left to
die in the flames.

I searched about me and found some
water, and in the twinkle of an eye
baptised him Christian as the rest
of us, *c'est bon!*
[*Delight then sorrow*]
I looked for where I might put him
safe out of the fire and God spoke;
it struck me, his parents pagan!

His baptism would go to the devil
did they come back.

I put him in his cot, and went back
to my men. The roof fell in.

BURIDAN
He perished?

LANDRY

Oui. But who was it laughed?
God laughed, because when Satan
poked in the ashes for his angel he
got his fingers burned on the hot
soul of a little Christian! *Oui?*

BURIDAN

Oui.
But tell me of a child give you by
Marguerite of Bourgogne.

LANDRY

You know of that?

BURIDAN

Tell me.

LANDRY

I will. Orsini, her creature, told
me, toss in the river like cats
are, forgive me, I did not.

I was tempted and I fell.

[*He tips the imaginary scales with his finger and laughs*]

BURIDAN

What did you do?

LANDRY

Took them to Notre Dame and exposed
them on the cobbles, Christian.

BURIDAN

[*Shaken*] Them?

LANDRY

Them. There were two, that they
were Christians I was sure...

BURIDAN

What became of them?

LANDRY

They were taken. In the evening
they were gone.

Poor little mites, I hope one day
to meet them again and dandle them
on my knee.

[*BURIDAN asks urgently, hoarsely:*]

BURIDAN

How will you know them?

LANDRY

A sharp knife. I cut them, deep in
the arm, Christians, with a cross.

How they screamed, but it was for
the best.

[*BURIDAN has gone cold with horror*]

BURIDAN

Which arm?

LANDRY

The left arm, each one.

BURIDAN

My sons!

One dead, the other about to be, both,
by her and by me!
[*Shatters hour glass*]
Landry, a boat.

I must reach the Tower of Nesle
before that young man I have sent
to his death.

Where is there a boat, who?

LANDRY

Simon, the fisherman.

BURIDAN
Then your sword, and follow me.

LANDRY
Where, *capitaine?*

BURIDAN
A la Tour de Nesle, malheureux!

[*Exit BURIDAN, followed by LANDRY*]

[*Music*]

SCENE 7

The river Seine. Banks
Night

[*BURIDAN and LANDRY in the boat. GAULTIER on the banks, through mist and the skulking denizens of Paris*]

[*Music*]

SCENE 8

The Tower of Nesle
Night

[*Music. Discovered MARGUERITE and ORSINI. ORSINI at the window*]

MARGUERITE
This man knows all we hope secret,
life, death, thine, mine, Orsini.
But I contest his will these three
days, we would be in his power.

That he prevails not is remarkable.

ORSINI
The devil tells him, is at his
orders - he knows all that we do.

MARGUERITE
With a word did he force me on my
knees like a slave.
By devil wiles he had me release
his bonds, cord by cord.
Then had he the impertinence to
demand of me - all!

All, Orsini, this night!

ORSINI
But him, none other?

MARGUERITE
But him, it is a last necessity,
but him.

ORSINI
Signora. Do but command me, I shall
be the first to order "Kill him!"

But... dare I ask, shall I say...

MARGUERITE
What dare you?

ORSINI
In what respect do I prosper, these
nights? How? Give me gain? Did I
not... what?

[*MARGUERITE is taken aback*]

MARGUERITE
Ah, it must be done, Orsini, you
know well it must.

You also want him dead, you would
kill yea or nay for your own peace
of mind would you not?

ORSINI

For he knows what he knows I would,
this last time - not ever again.

I tire, and I do not extravagantly
prosper.

The sins pile, but little else.
[*Piously*]
We must try cleanse our souls for
our eternal rest, our heaven bane.

MARGUERITE

While he lives I am not queen, not
mistress of my wealth, my treasure,
not even my life but with him dead.
[*Angry*] I swear it you, no more of it
[*She succumbs*]
Not only this but I shall give you
gold, as much would buy a province.

This tower shall be rased. I shall
build a convent of its evil stones.

I shall found a community of friars
will pass their days at prayer bare
foot on the bare stones.

They will be ordered pray for me and...
[*Almost a threat*]
...pray for you, Orsini.

I am as tired as you are of these
sordid couplings, these deaths...

[*Shocking thought*] I fear!

The thought occurs that God is
poised to pardon me only if I do
not carry out this one last death!

ORSINI

No no, it is just, he knows all, he
is lost. How comes he?

MARGUERITE

By those stairs.

ORSINI

I shall place my men.

MARGUERITE

Listen!
[*To the window*] What is it?

ORSINI

A boat rowed by two men.

MARGUERITE

It is him.

Go, there is no time to lose. Go!
Lock the door that I am safe from
him, he even now... may surprise us.
Go, go! Secure me in against. him.

[*Exit ORSINI. The door slammed boomingly shut, the key turned*]

Gaultier! This is he would keep us
apart.

He wanted gold, I gave it, honours,
I gave them...

Did you but know how much he wishes
us apart you would pardon me his
death...

Gaultier, this man is evil, this
Lyonnet, this Buridan!

And he is being sent back to the
hell from which he came! It is he
who must bear my guilt, it is he
who made me spill so much blood!

God is just, all blame will fall on
him, and me, oh me, me!

Were I my judge, I would not dare
to expect absolution.

[*Listening at the door*]
It has not begun, I hear nothing yet,
nothing...

[*Enter BURIDAN through the window*]

BURIDAN
Marguerite! Marguerite! Alone!
God be praised!

MARGUERITE
A moi! A moi, Orsini!

BURIDAN
Fear nothing!

MARGUERITE
You!

BURIDAN
Marguerite, there is something you
must know...

MARGUERITE
What more will you demand of me?

BURIDAN
Nothing... see...
[*Tossing them from him*]
...Far from me, my sword, far from
me my dagger, far from me this box,
in which are all our secrets.

Now, you may kill me, I am not
armed, I am without armour. Kill
me, take the box, burn the letter
you will find within and sleep
tranquil on my grave.

I come not to do you ill, I have
come to speak...

Oh, did you but know what I have
come to tell you!

It is that which will bring back
those days of happiness, to us,
though we are cruelly cursed...

MARGUERITE
I don't understand.

BURIDAN
Marguerite have you nothing in your
heart womanly, naught of a mother?
Is she, I have known once so pure,
now, without that which is sacred
both to God and man?

MARGUERITE
Talk to me, of purity and virtue,
you!

Satan is converted!

BURIDAN
Marguerite have you never for one
moment repented?

Answer me as you would answer God
for I can offer you happiness or
despair, I can damn you or absolve
you, I can offer heaven or hell.

Can you not confess to me all you
have suffered?

MARGUERITE
There is no priest I would dare
confess to, not one. Only to
someone bears guilt equal to mine
might I confess.

You, Buridan, you Lyonnet.

But for you that young girl would
not have killed her father, would
not have lost her sons, you alone

bear guilt with me, and to you
alone can I speak of it...

Driven by remorse I sought to sate
conscience in pleasure and blood.

None bade me stop, none bade me
remember virtue.

From the mouths of courtiers came
naught but smiles.

They whispered me I was beautiful,
the world was mine, I could by
crook of finger turn everything
upside down was it my pleasure.

Without strength of conscience to
resist came a swoon of passion,
drunken remorse, dreams a'swirl
with ghosts, sensuous... pain.

Oui.

Only to one as guilty as I am could
I tell these things.

                    BURIDAN
Tell me if... what... had you,
your sons?

                    MARGUERITE
Oh!

Then, oh I dare not, could not, not
if I... no, I dare not think of it.

But I could not keep my sons.

[*She whispers*]

My sons. I cannot say the words
for among the ghosts haunt me night
after night, not once have they
come, they who most of all should,
and it is a delicate balanced world
that of nightmare, my misplaced
words could evoke their shadows!

BURIDAN

Marguerite, they have been close to
you.

MARGUERITE

Close?

BURIDAN

One of them, on his knees, asked
for mercy... you were there, you
heard him plead...

MARGUERITE

I... when, where?

BURIDAN

Here, this room, you.

MARGUERITE

When?

BURIDAN

He was with me, that night.

MARGUERITE

Philippe d'Aulnay. I struck! You lie!

BURIDAN

No. You struck!

MARGUERITE

I struck... him. What proof?

BURIDAN

None. The word of a villainous
sergeant... what is that?

His word, he took them, marked them
with a cross, laid them front of
Notre Dame - to die or to be taken.

MARGUERITE

If it is true...?

BURIDAN

It is true.

[*MARGUERITE looks hard at him, realises, accepts, is overcome, horrified*]

MARGUERITE

Vengeance de Dieu! I it was struck
him... dead.

BURIDAN

Oh bitter... and... there is another.

[*MARGUERITE groans, nods*]

MARGUERITE

Gaultier!

BURIDAN

The lover of his mother! Taste of
this...!

MARGUERITE

No, thank God... no, by heaven's
grace not so, on my knees I thank
God... I still can call Gaultier
my son, he may call me...!

BURIDAN

Is it true?

MARGUERITE

By the blood spilled here I can
swear!It was the hand of God
that reached out, a strange
love, never that of a lover, always
that of a mother... it was God...

The good God, the saviour who will
have joy and repentance come back
into my life... *mon Dieu, merci,
merci.*

[*Down on her knees she prays*]

BURIDAN

Marguerite. Do you forgive me? Are
we no longer enemies?

MARGUERITE
No, you are the father of Gaultier,
my remaining son.

BURIDAN
Our son is he who binds us, in
terrible secrecy... what we have
done... and...
Oh you struck...

MARGUERITE
I struck...!

BURIDAN
... and... love?

MARGUERITE
Oui, oui. Love.

BURIDAN
Do you believe we can be... happy
again?

MARGUERITE
I do believe it!

BURIDAN
All we need is our son.

MARGUERITE
Our son, here with us.

BURIDAN
He comes.

MARGUERITE
Here?

BURIDAN
He has the key you gave me.

MARGUERITE
Then he comes through the postern!

BURIDAN
He does.

[*MARGUERITE screams:*]

MARGUERITE

Then he is a dead man!

For that way *you* were to come!

[*Cries heard off:* "A moi! A moi! Au secours!"]

BURIDAN

It is he they murder!

[*BURIDAN tries to open door. Throws himself against it*]

MARGUERITE

The door is locked. Gaultier!
Orsini! Orsini!

[*BURIDAN hammers on door with the hilt of his sword*]

BURIDAN

Open this door!

MARGUERITE

I have not the key.

BURIDAN

Then he is dead?

[*MARGUERITE collapses, sobs*]

MARGUERITE

He is... dead. Our son.

BURIDAN

The door opens!

[*Enter GAULTIER covered in blood*]

GAULTIER

Marguerite... I give you back the
key to the Tower...

MARGUERITE

Gaultier, I am your mother.

GAULTIER

My mother? My mother?

[*Horror - his hand and arm out to curse her*]
    Then be damned!

[*GAULTIER dies*]

[*BURIDAN down on knees, tugs at the dead man's sleeve*]

BURIDAN

His arm, Landry marked his arm.

Oui. It is there, the mark of the
cross.

Our sons damned in the womb of
their mother!

A murder at their birth, a murder
cut down their life.

MARGUERITE

Pity, pity!

[*Enter ORSINI*]

[*Enter SAVOISY with the GUARDS. ORSINI denounces:*]

ORSINI

Monseigneur. Here are they who are
the real murderers, they, not I.

SAVOISY

You are my prisoners.

BURIDAN/MARGUERITE

Prisoners? We?

MARGUERITE

I, the queen?

BURIDAN

I, first minister?

SAVOISY

I see here no queen, no minister.

There is the murdered body of my
friend.

There two assassins.

Here an order signed by the king to arrest this night all found in the Tower of Nesle, whatever rank or title!

BURIDAN

Commend me to God!

MARGUERITE

Amen, His mercy.

[*Flames of Hell lick. Consume them*]

[*Music*]

Curtain

Fin de La Tour De Nesle

www.ingramcontent.com/pod-product-compliance
Ingram Content Group UK Ltd.
Pitfield, Milton Keynes, MK11 3LW, UK
UKHW031253020325
455690UK00007B/56

9 781870 259606